UKULELE
Design & Construction

A comprehensive guide to construct a Hawaiian Tenor Ukulele

Step by step instructions for
Spanish Style and Box Style Construction
For All Woodworker

By D. Henry Wickham

All photography and drawings by Author

Second Edition
2006

Order this book online at www.trafford.com
or email orders@trafford.com

Most Trafford titles are also available at major online book retailers.

© Copyright 2004 D. Henry Wickham.
All rights reserved. No part of this publication may be reproduced, stored in a retrieval system, or transmitted, in any form or by any means, electronic, mechanical, photocopying, recording, or otherwise, without the written prior permission of the author.

Print information available on the last page.

ISBN: 978-1-4120-3909-3 (sc)

Because of the dynamic nature of the Internet, any web addresses or links contained in this book may have changed since publication and may no longer be valid. The views expressed in this work are solely those of the author and do not necessarily reflect the views of the publisher, and the publisher hereby disclaims any responsibility for them.

Any people depicted in stock imagery provided by Getty Images are models, and such images are being used for illustrative purposes only.
Certain stock imagery © Getty Images.

Trafford rev. 06/27/2019

 www.trafford.com

North America & international
toll-free: 844-688-6899 (USA & Canada)
fax: 812 355 4082

UKULELE Design & Construction

Dedicated to the memory of

Champion My Molly Mo
1994-2002

and to George.....

*Thanks George! Thank you for so many years of beautiful music and your profound place in history.
All who know you love you*

Contents

CHAPTER 1 *Wood* 6

CHAPTER 2 *Preparing the Soundboard & Back* 9

CHAPTER 3 *The Rosette* 18

CHAPTER 4 *Bracing the Soundboard & Back* 23

CHAPTER 5 *Sides* 28

CHAPTER 6 *Necks* 36

CHAPTER 7 *Fretboard* 62

CHAPTER 8 *Assembly I* 74

CHAPTER 9 *End Graft* 96

CHAPTER 10 *Bridge* 101

CHAPTER 11 *Locating Bridge* 106

CHAPTER 12 *Binding* 109

CHAPTER 13 *Finishing* 115

CHAPTER 14 *Tuning Machines, Nut & Saddle* 118

CHAPTER 15 *Set-up* 120

Jigs & Plans 122

Bill of Materials 136

Source of Supplies 137

Fret Scale 138

The Ukulele's Anatomy 139

PREFACE

Welcome! You are about to embark on a wonderful woodworking journey. This book shares suggestions that I have discovered over 35 years, and as recent as yesterday. What is most important are the many mistakes that I have made over the years. They gave me a permanent reminder of what not to do. I hope that you can view this book as a bundle of ideas and construction techniques as a guided discovery into the art of ukulele construction. This is only one person's view and is always subject to debate. I encourage you to combine woodworking and luthery methods from many sources. There has not been a great deal of information written on the subject of ukulele construction, but there is a world of information available on every stage of woodworking and finishing. There are excellent books on guitar construction listed in the resource section at the end of this book. I am hopeful that this book can answer some question and encourage you to build a "uke". Most of my experience is in building guitars and my approach to building a ukulele is as if they are little guitars.

It is beyond the scope of this book to instruct you on the subject of sharpening methods, finishing processes, or advanced woodworking techniques. This book will help guide you through the process to build a professional quality instrument.

Please remember this:
- use only SHARP tools
- don't forget the wax paper
- do not try to apply finish until conditions are right
- always sand to at lease 400 grit!

Every effort has been made to provide you with accurate information and precise dimensions. This book is one person's method and interpretation of the process of the construction of a ukulele. Any trade name or entity referred to in this book is for your convenience and I do not endorse nor do I receive any compensation from anyone for using or printing their names.

Anyone can build and enjoy a ukulele! This book is written with the first time builder in mind, but it contains some advanced applications.

Best of luck and don't forget your mistakes. Soon you will have a wonderful masterpiece of esthetic beauty and sonic excellence.

Chapter 1
Wood

When choosing wood for any stringed instrument it's structural properties and aesthetic qualities must be considered. Wood is a hydroscopic material and is subject to moisture changes. Wood will shrink or swell in response to environmental temperature and moisture. This reaction is known as *equilibrium moisture content* (EMC).

Because wood is so susceptible to it's environment, you should allow sufficient time for the wood to adjust to the conditions in which it is to be used. This is especially true for wood that comes from another part of the world as is often the case with exotic woods. If you order wood from Hawaii and it will be used in Alabama, you should let it sit open with free air movement for a while. Most wood that you buy from a luthier supply company has been properly air dried and usually safe to use soon after a short acclimation period.

Wood Storage

If you are able to buy wood for future use, you should do so. The more desirable wood used in ukulele construction is certain to become more valuable and some of the best wood has become endangered and no longer allowed to be cut. An example is Brazilian Rosewood. I view purchasing wood for instruments as an investment. It is a far better investment than many stocks!

Your collection of wood must be stored properly, even if you have only one set. Air must be able to circulate freely and remain in a controlled environment that is close to 50% relative humidity and no hotter than 75 to 80 degrees. Store it this way until you start construction.

Your rough or joined and sanded plate should be stored horizontally on "stickers". Stickers are small 3/8 X 3/8 inch straight and flat strips of softwood. Spruce, fir or white pine are good. Stack your wood with a pair of stickers between each piece of your soundboards, backs and sides. You must line up the stickers so that they are directly above the one below. The top piece of your stack of wood can be a ¼ inch piece of plywood with a light weight on top. This will allow proper air circulation and help to keep you wood flat and allow the wood to move as it is air dried. See **Photo 1-1**.

(**Photo 1-1**) Wood air drying for future use. Some are rough blanks and some are glued and sanded to thickness. *Stickers* separate the plates.

When choosing wood for any stringed instrument, structural properties and esthetic qualities should be considered. Wood that is sawn perpendicular to the annual growth rings is known to be quartersawn or riff sawn. Quartersawn wood is the most stable and has very tight and straight grain on the face of the board. Quartersawn wood dramatically enhances acoustic qualities as well as it's beauty. Careful resawing can create spectacular and dramatic *curly* or *fiddleback* rays. Koa wood is a prime example of beauty and good physical qualities. It is my first choice for ukulele construction. Sitka spruce and Engelman spruce make a good choice for the soundboard.

Some Hawaiian species for ukuleles:
--Koa
--Mango
--Pheasantwood
--Ohia
--Milo

Other hardwoods for ukuleles:
--Honduran mahogany
--Brazilian rosewood
--East Indian Rosewood
--Lacewood

Soundboards:
--Sitka spruce
--Engelman spruce
--Alaskan Yellow cedar

Necks:
--Honduran mahogany
--Quarter sawn maple
--Bird's Eye maple

(**Photo 1-2**) Resawing thick stock to make back plates. Each will be sawn to make ample thickness for joining the back halves and sanding out all of the saw marks. Saw the back plates and tops to a minimum thickness of ¼ inch to allow joining and final sanding.

(**Photo 1-3**) The mark on edge of thick board being resawn will allow the thin plates to stack up book-matched.

End of Chapter 1

Chapter 2
Preparing the Soundboard & Back

Procedure: Preparing the soundboard and back plates:

At this point, the procedure is the same for preparing the soundboard and back. Select a pair of bookmatched top plates & back plates. They should be no smaller than 5 X 14 inches. You must end up with a joined plate no smaller than 10 X 14 inches. Bigger is better so you can avoid any defects in the wood. The final sanded thickness of the top will be 0.125 inches or about 1/8 inch. The back and sides after final thickness sanding will be .095 inches or about 3/32 inch. Keep this in mind as you mill your wood. If you are building your ukulele from a kit, everything may be sanded for you. Some dimensions may be slightly thinner for mahogany kits. It is most essential that you work from professionally drawn plans of a proven design. (See *Sources of Supplies*)

Step 1: Using the plates described above, the edges must be strait and true. The edges can be prepared with a joiner, edge sander or shooting board. We will use the shooting board. See below.

(**Photo 2-1**)   Simple shooting board used to prepare sides for gluing.

The large sanding block has 120 grit sandpaper glued to one side. The wood for the sanding block must be dead square to the table. Many times a block plane is used instead of a sanding block. See section on *Jigs* for detailed instructions.

(**Photo 2-2**) A beautiful example of a bookmatched curly Koa plate

Determine the bookmatched edges and fold the sides together using the marked edges as a guide. Place the two halves together on the shooting board and clamp. Using a sanding block 10 inches long, 120 grit sandpaper, sand the edges of the plates in pairs using the shooting board as a guide. When the edges are sanded, hold the joint up to the light and check the fit. If you see any light repeat the process.

Step 2: Gluing the Two Halves Together

Using the edge gluing jig, position one of the halves against the wooden guide strip. Place a strip of wax paper under the joint. Place the other half plate against the first plate. Adjust the movable wooden guide to a position where there is enough room for the clamping wedges to fit between the guide and the plate being glued. Clamp the movable guide at this position. Each of the two pairs of small wooden wedges are pressed together so as to push the two half plates together. Once adjusted and the movable guide is clamped, apply a line of glue and smooth with finger. Use enough glue to adequately cover the edges. Clamp as described for now. We will add a caul above the glue joint. First cover with wax paper and clamp a 2 inch wide piece of ¾ plywood directly over the joint. This will keep the joint level. Allow to dry two hours minimum. The wax paper slows down the drying process, so allow extra time. See **Photo 2-3**

(**Photo 2-3**) Plate Gluing Jig. Notice the small wooden wedges at the back and the caul across the center seam. The two extra clamps in the front corners are just used to keep the bottom board level.

(**Photo 2-4**) A close up detail of the opposing small wooden wedges that serve to clamp the two half plates together.

(**Photo 2-5**) You can add a backstrip to the back as you glue the two halves together. This is a 1/16 wide Black-White-Black purfling. If you have somewhat plain wood that you are working with this may add some interest. A vivid bookmatched back dose not need any help. The soundboard never has an inlay strip. If any of your joints are not perfectly joined now is the time to fix the problem.

Simply rip the plate in half and start over. Go back to the shooting board stage. Most of the problems with joining the plates are the backstrips. Also, sometimes the halves do not lay flat during clamping. At this point you do not have much extra wood thickness to sand the problem away. Just rip it and start over.

Step 3: Sanding the plates to thickness

Once the soundboard and back a safely dry lay then flat with stickers between each plate (see photo 1-1) Cover the to pair of stickers with a piece of plywood and put something of medium weight on the plywood and set aside. After a day the plates can safely sanded to thickness.

Sanding the plates will require a thicknessing sander. Many cabinet shops have this machine. If you buy your wood form a luthier supply house they may join, glue and sand your soundboard and back for you if you buy the material from them.

(**Photo 2-6**) A soundboard being sanded to proper thickness. The glue line is sanded away and the soundboard is sanded to a thickness of 1/8 inch.

To have the soundboard glued and sanded it is about $15 and to have the back glued and sides sanded it is around $25. (See *Source of Supplies*) I know of many instruments that had their soundboards and backs planed to thickness with hand planes. I will admit this is a huge task but it has been done for hundreds of years. I will freely admit this process is far beyond my ability. As we learned earlier, the final thickness of the soundboard will be about 1/8 inch. The final thickness of the back and sides will be about 3/32 inch.

Step 4: Layout the pattern of the soundboard

It is advisable to glue the paper patterns from your plan to poster board or other thick paper using spray glue. You will use the pattern several times during construction. A thicker pattern may allow you to make more exact measurements.

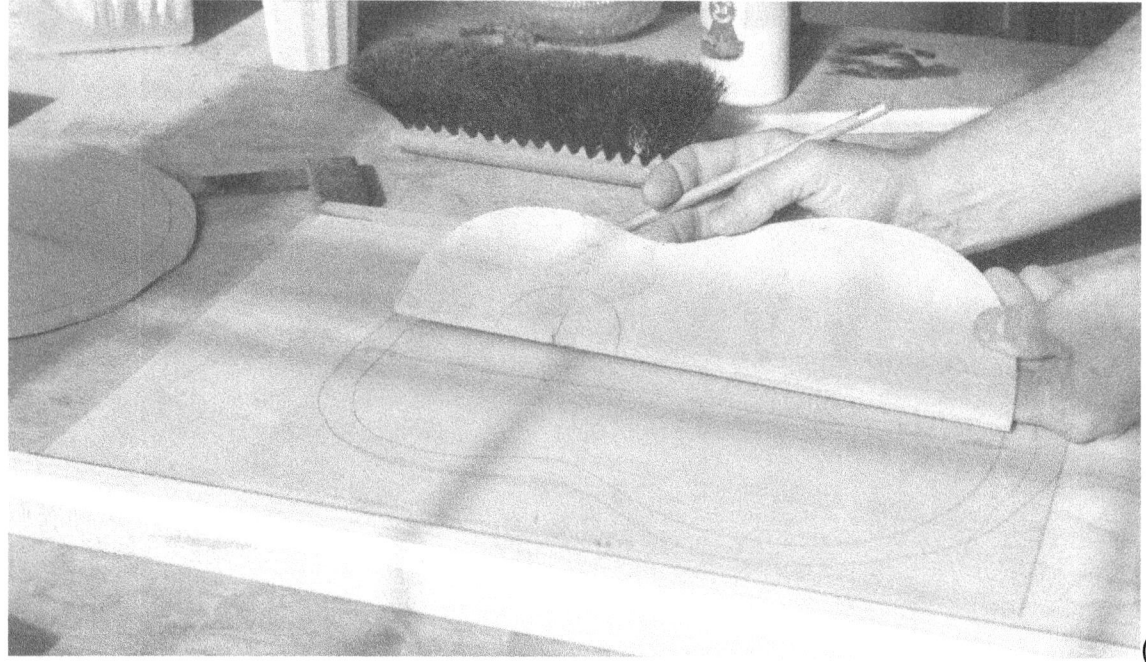

Photo 2-7) Lay out the outline using half templates to assure symmetry

Lay out the outline of the pattern from your plans- (see Source of Supplies) or from the layout included in this book. It would be many times easier to work from professional plans rather than just guessing. Everything is where it is and how big it is for a very good reason.

Start by marking a centerline on the back of the soundboard and the back. It should be exactly on the center seam. The centerline will be referred to throughout the construction process and all measurements should be made from these centerlines. This will reduce the chance for error in your measurements and reduce the need for elaborate calculations. Layout the soundboard pattern on the bottom of the plate. For now the only mark needed on the top side is the exact center of the soundhole. This is done after everything is marked and checked for accuracy. Just drill a 3/16 inch hole through the soundboard from the back side. This will locate the exact center of the soundhole and the rosette.

Transfer the locations of the braces by punching a small hole in the center of each end of the braces on your paper pattern. Lay your paper pattern on the back of the soundboard and make pencil point marks at the holes. With a sharp lead pencil just connect all of the dots. Draw your lines slightly longer than the pattern so you can see the lines clearly when the braces are in place. Once you have the braces laid out it is time to cut the soundboard and back to an oversize shape. Draw a second line about ½ inch on the outside of the line of the pattern of the soundboard and back plates. See **Photo 2-7**.

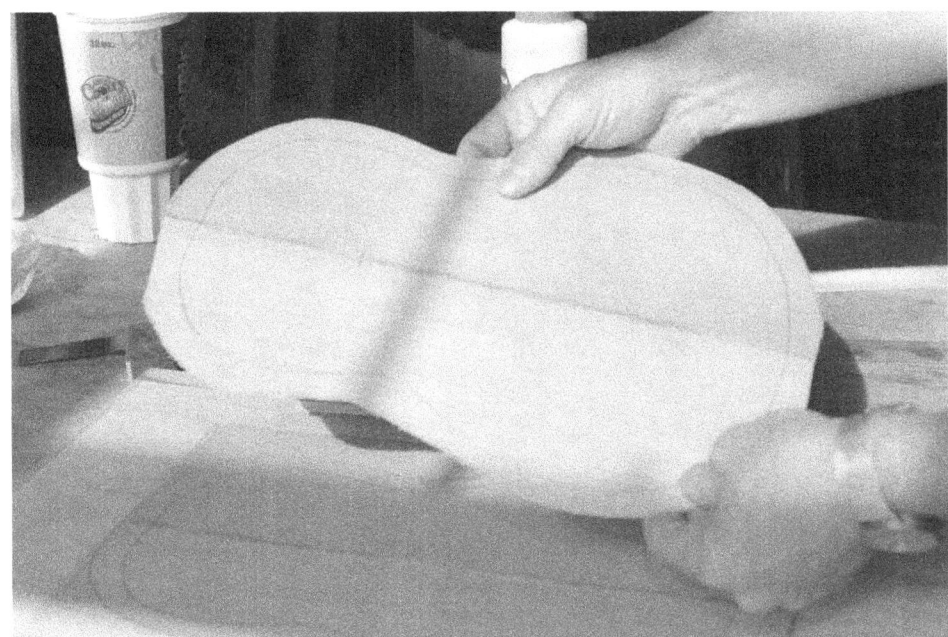

(Photo 2-8) The soundboard is cut to oversize shape and is ready for the bracing layout. One of the ukuleles we are building for this book is all mahogany, top, back, sides and neck. Here you see soundboard and back.

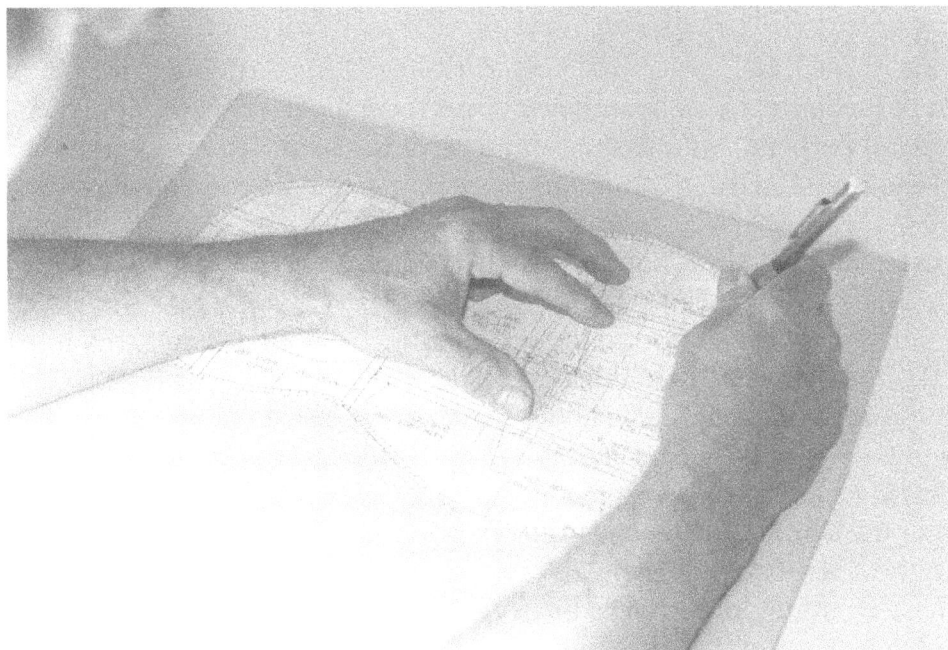

(Photo 2-9) Marking the centerline points of brace layout. Next the lines are drawn to connect points.

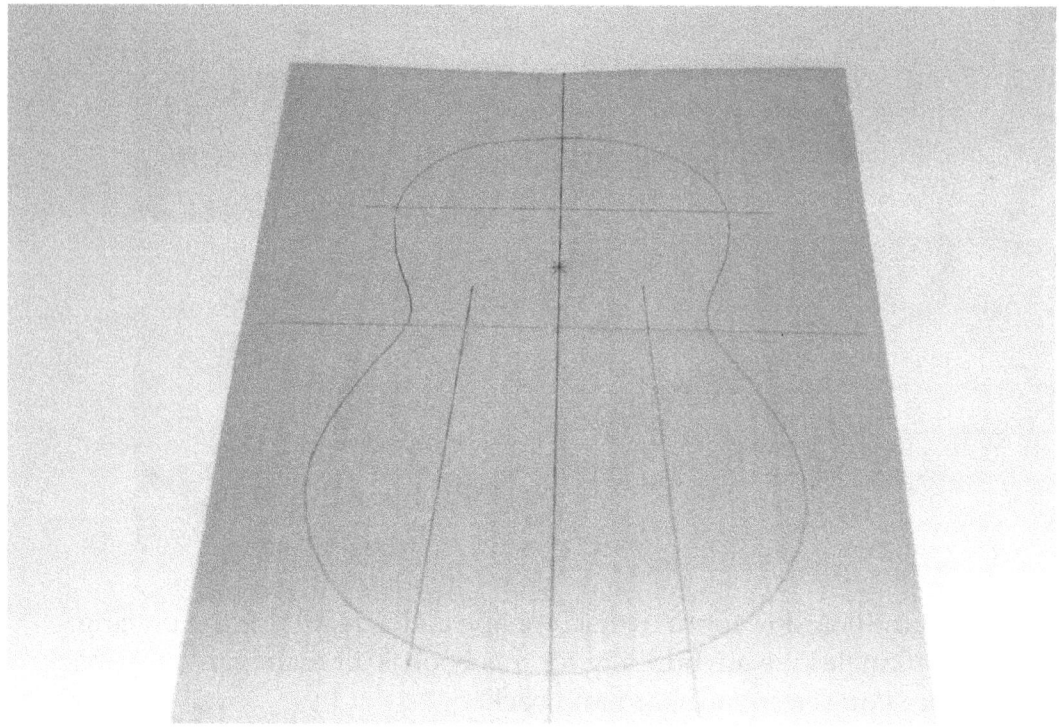

(**Photo 2-10**) Braces marked on the back of the soundboard. A 3/16 hole drilled at the center point of the sound hole.

The layout of the back braces is similar to soundboard. The back has only three braces and they are all perpendicular to the centerline of the back. The back plate can be laid aside until the soundboard is complete. Store it in a climate controlled environment.

Step 5: Cutting and installing sound hole patch

Before we can cut anything around the sound hole, the sound hole patch must be installed. This is a piece of 1/16 thick mahogany (or whatever the type wood you are using for your soundboard) that is glued between the waist bar and the upper waist bar. (refer to your plans) The patch has a outside diameter of 3 ¾ inches and the soundhole will be 2 ½ in diameter. Since none of the braces have been glued, the placement of the sound hole patch is very important. The diameter of the patch is wider than the space between the waist bars so it must be cut to fit between the two braces. These cuts should be marked before the patch is cut into a circle and must be parallel. Also locate and drill a 3/16 hole to match the hole in the soundboard at the center of the sound hole. This step is very important so be accurate. Glue and clamp patch using two cam clamps with a caul. Allow to dry one hour.

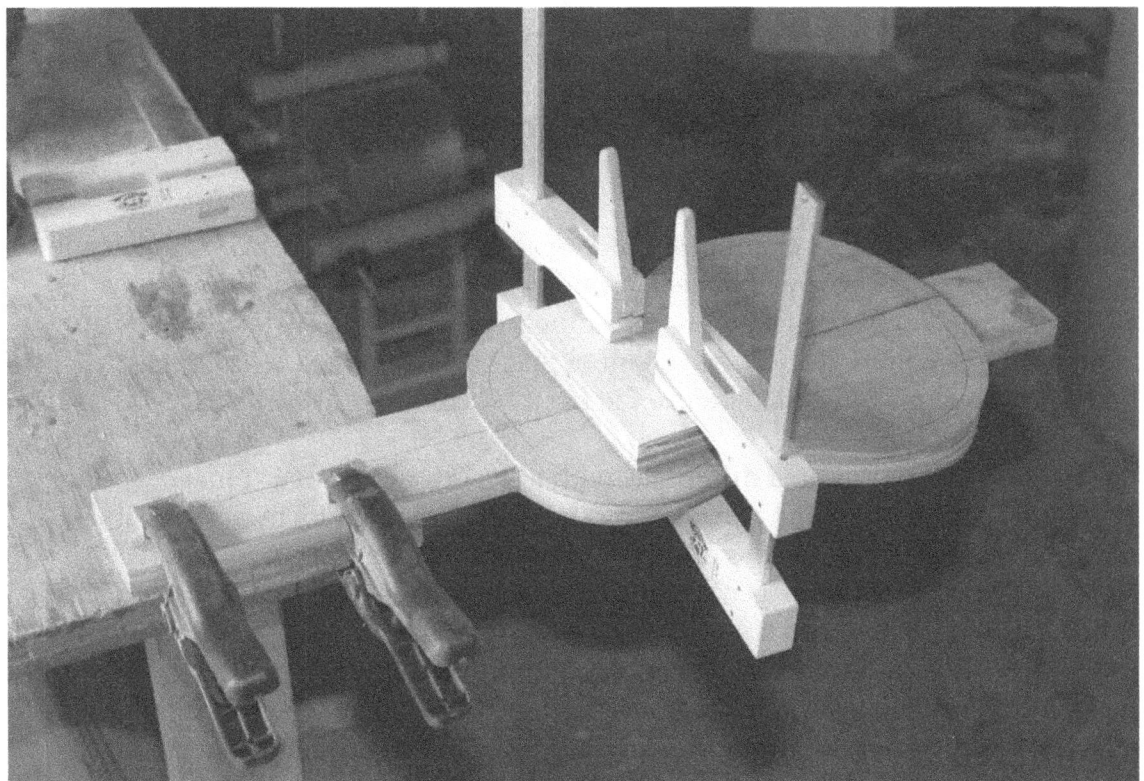

(Photo 2-11) Soundhole patch being glued to the back of the soundboard. Notice the assembly jig. It allows you to gain access all of the way around the assembly.

End of Chapter 2

Chapter 3
The Rosette

Step 1: Cutting channels for the rosette

Many ukuleles do not have rosettes but we will add one to our ukulele. The inner diameter of the first channel should be approximately 3 inches at the inside diameter. The soundhole will have a diameter of 2 ½ inches. Rosettes can consist of several separate channels and sometime become very detailed but our rosette will have only one 1/8 inch channel that will be inlayed with paua shell. The rosette is usually installed before the front braces are glued into place.

The channels can be cut on a drill press with a flycutter or with a router. Special cutters are required to cut the grooves on the drill press. Confirm the size of your inlay material and adjust your inlay channels as necessary width and height. A Dremel tool with a circle cutting attachment is a very good tool for the channels as well as the thru cut for the soundhole. I use a flycutter for the final thru cut for the soundhole. The channels are cut first and the soundhole last. The soundboard will need to be shimmed up the thickness of the soundhole patch for the cuts to be accurate. Locate the shims to even out the soundboard on your work surface.

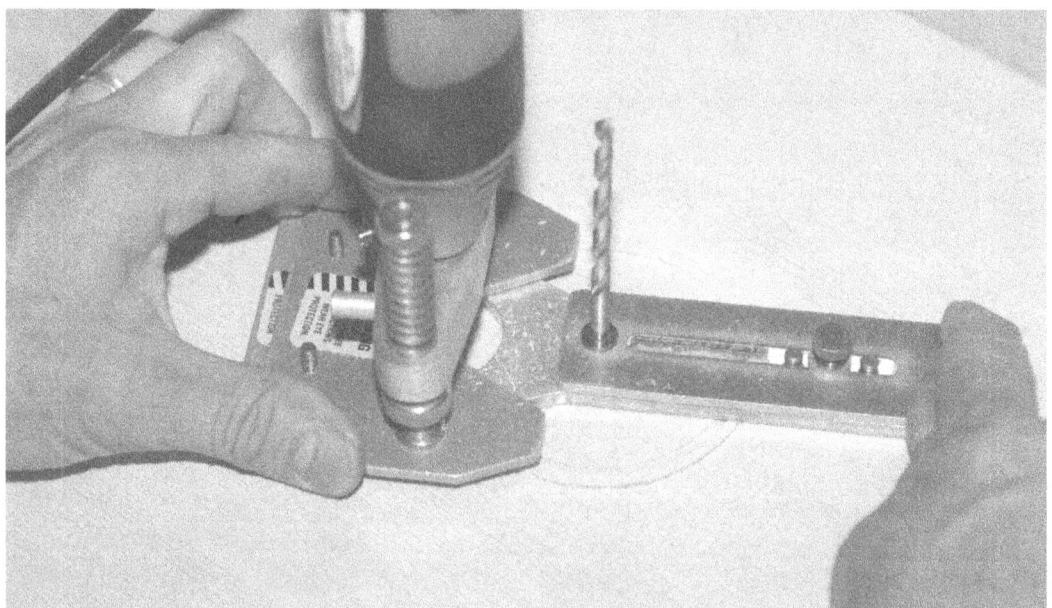

(Photo 3-1) Channels are cut into soundboard with a Dremel tool and a 1/8 inch and 1/16 inch downcut router bit. Be sure to confirm the depth of your inlay material. Do not cut the channels too deep. The drill bit is being used to align the 3/16 inch holes in the soundboard and a circle cutting attachment.

Step 2: Cutting the soundhole

(Photo 3-2) Cutting the sound hole with a flycutter. The cutter uses a ¼ inch drill bit as a guide and it is used at a slow speed on your drill press.

The cutter that comes with most flycutters is designed to cut a hole in material with the side of the cut to be perpendicular to the material. You can get cutter blanks and grind you own cutters. It is good practice to cut thru the top and only part of the soundhole patch. After you have cut about 75% from the top, turn the soundboard over and finish cutting the hole from the back side. This helps to reduce the chance of tear out as the cutter exits the wood.

Another way to cut the soundhole is to use the small router with a circle cutting attachment similar to the process of cutting the inlay channel. You must make several cuts, deeper each time, to successfully cut the soundhole with a small (1/16 inch) router bit. (See Photo 3-1) If soundhole is cut with a small downcut router bit, the inlay channels and soundhole can be cut at the same time.

Step 3: Rosette Inlay

The rosette for this book is a very simple one. Many rosettes are very complicated mosaic made up of hundreds of pieces like those found on classical guitars. Ukulele rosettes are usually much more simple, sometimes consisting of only one or two inlay channels. We will use 1/8 inch abalone inlay material that has be cut into a circle that has an inside diameter of 3 inches. A 1/8 inch downcut router bit was used in a Dremel tool with a circle cutting attachment to cut the inlay channel. Make the adjustments to the router bit and circle cutting attachment and test on a scrap piece of wood.

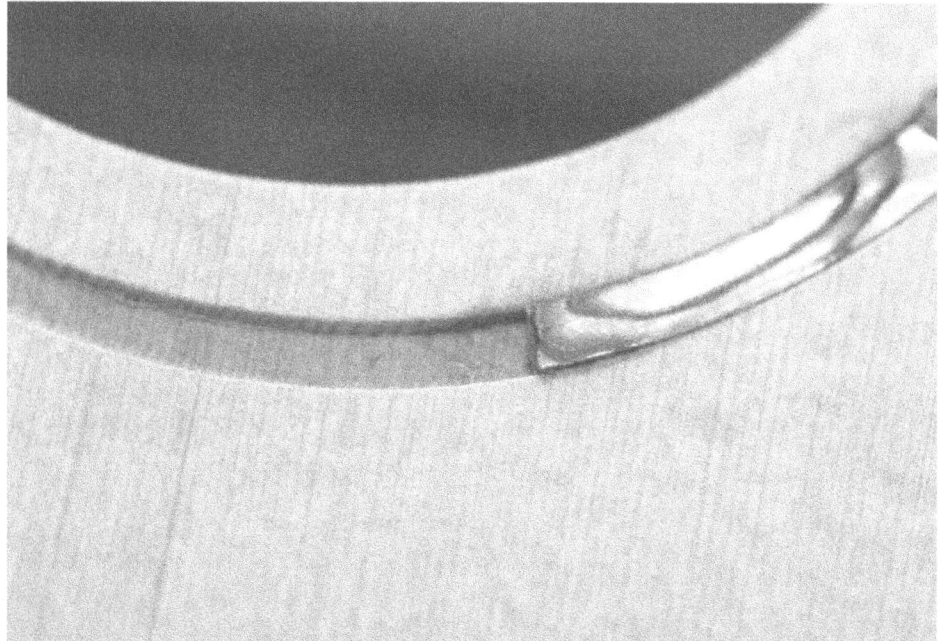
(**Photo 3-3**) Checking the fit of the inlay material in rosette channel

Test fit the width of the inlay channel. The inlay material should fit snugly but not tight. The inlay material is very fragile and should be handled with care. Do not be concerned if a piece is broken because you can glue the two pieces in the channel without much evidence of the break.

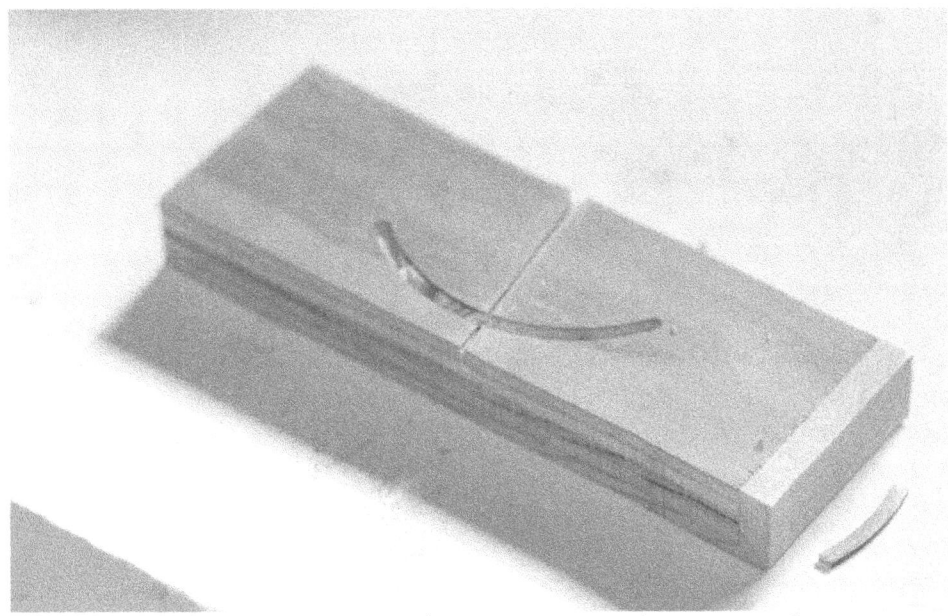

(**Photo 3-4**) A simple jig to mitre inlay material

(**Photo 3-5**) Cutting inlay strips with mitre jig

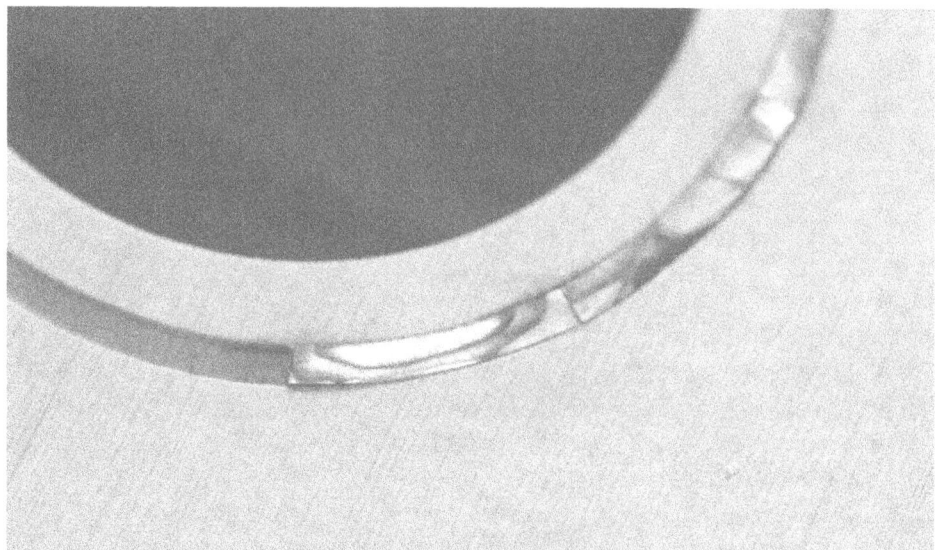

(Photo 3-6) Inlay being glued in channel. Mitres match perfectly with use of jig.

(**Photo 3-7**) Rosette inlay complete

The glue used to glue most inlay is a medium thickness Cyano glue. A chemical accelerator is available to make the glue set instantly for delicate work. The same glue is used for many things in ukulele building. It is a good idea to have thin and medium Cyano glue and accelerator on hand. It comes in black also. (see *Source of Supplies*)

End of Chapter 3

Chapter 4
Bracing the Soundboard & Back

The wood used for bracing the soundboard and back is called bracewood. Really. Most bracewood is quartersawn Sitka spruce or quartersawn mahogany because of the consistent grain pattern and strength. When you buy bracewood from luthier supply houses you get a unit of measure called a billet. A billet is usually about 1 ½ X 1 ½ X 22-24 inches. Spruce usually comes in billets thinner and wider. It is most important that you use quality bracewood because the wood, shape, and size contribute to much of the instrument's quality of sound. The size and shape of the braces are taken from your plans. Most ukulele braces start out as 1/4 inch X 3/8 inch. This book is based on a fan braced ukulele.

(**Photo 4-1**) Patterns of top braces and brace material cut to length.

Since the soundboard is flat, the bottom of the top braces are also flat. The braces taper towards each end with a highpoint at a calculated position, not always the middle of the brace. (See Plan) Once the soundboard braces are shaped they can be glued to the soundboard. Align each brace over the pencil lines drawn earlier and confirm all lengths and that the correct brace is where it is supposed to be. Use enough Titebond to cover but not an excessive amount. You want a very small amount of glue to be squeezed out under clamp pressure

(**Photo 4-2**) The braces glued in place in a fan shape

The three fan braces are shaped on a belt sander to a rough shape. They should be sanded to somewhat of a point at the top of each brace and tapered to about 1/16 inch where they meet the soundboard. The bout and upper bout braces are also somewhat domed or pointed and have a one inch + long scallop on each end. The braces should be finished off with a sharp wood chisel to a thickness of 1/16 inch at the end of the brace. Notice soundhole patch and layout lines.

The back of the ukulele will have an arch based on 15 foot radius. **Photo 4-3** illustrates the arch in the back braces. Some of the arch can be done on a belt sander, the rest is done a sanding block that has a curvature of 15 feet. This sanding block is essential in obtaining the proper radius in each of the three back braces. See *Jigs* section for more information

(**Photo 4-3**) A view of the back brace patterns and sized stock cut to length.

(**Photo 4-4**) 15 foot radius sanding board with 120 grit sandpaper

This sanding block is easily made by cutting the radius on the wide side of a 2X4. With the 2X4 on edge, extend a tape measure a distance of 15 feet and hook the end of the tape measure to a nail. With a pencil simply draw an arc with the pencil held at the 15 foot mark. Cut to shape on a band saw or sabre saw. Sand slightly to even the blade marks and stick self adhesive 120 grit sandpaper to the curved side.

Since the back is arched, the back braces must be glued with the clamps clamped to the brace and to the back itself. It cannot be clamped to a workboard because it will flatten the back arch. Clamp each brace with four clamps, one on each end and two in the middle. See sections on *Jigs*.

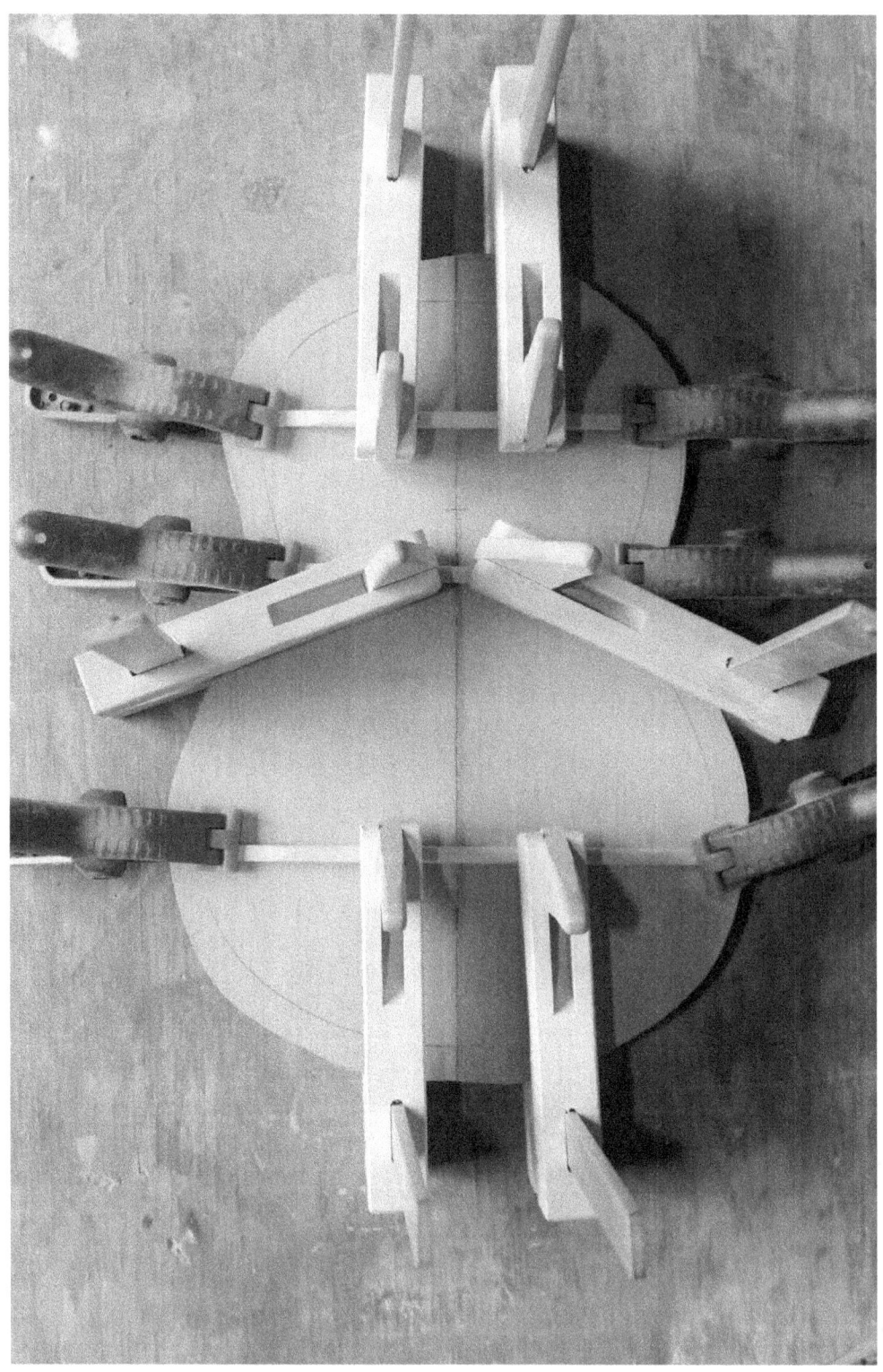

(Photo 4-5) Back braces glued and clamped.

(**Photo 4-6**) Close-up view of the back reinforcement strip

The seam where the back halves are joined is often times braced with aback joint reinforcement strip. It is usually cross-grained spruce and is glued in place, sanded and shaped before the back braces are glued into place. This allows for a very straight seam and a very tight fit to the back braces. The locations of the back braces are carefully marked and the spruce strip is simply cut and chiseled away to allow for the back braces. You will see this reinforcement strip in less than 75% of the newer ukuleles made and usually only on tenor and baritone ukuleles. The back braces help hold the two half plates of the back.

(**Photo 4-7**) Soundboard and Back with braces glued in place. Notice the back joint reinforcement on the back. It is more important when you have a center strip inlay in the back.

Now is a good time to sign and date the bottom of the soundboard and back.

Chapter 5
Sides

Procedure: Layout and cutting sides to size for bending

The sides will come bookmatched just like the soundboard and the back plates. The wood for the sides should be the same as the wood used for the back. The minimum size for each side piece is 3 1/2 X 22 inches and 3/32 inch thick. Use care in laying out the sides because there is a right side and a left side. The back will have a taper and you can will save a much work and time by cutting this taper when you can work with flat wood rather than wood that has been bent and glued to a heel block and a end block.

Step 1: Layout

Determine the sides and edge that is a book-match and prepare the two sides using edge sander or shooting board. Next tape the two sides together on the jointed side. Transfer the dimensions directly to the sides or make a pattern from poster board or 1/4 inch plywood.

(**Photo 5-1**) Preparing one edge of each side using shooting board

The length of the sides of a Spanish style neck is 18 inches and for a Boxstyle neck is ½ inch longer. One end of the sides is 3 inches wide and the other end is 2 ¾ inches. Make a mark at the waist line which is the center point of where the ukulele body curves into the body. This measurement is very important because it will become a reference point when we bend the sides. For this instrument it is 7 inches from the end that is 2 ¾ inches wide. From the jointed edges draw a square pencil line across the sides using a square. Next we will calculate the highest point on the sides. This will build in the taper necessary. On most guitars and ukuleles the high point is 2 inches behind the waist line and ¼ to 3/8 of an inch taller than the tail end (3 inch end). Our side will be 3 ¼ inches tall.

Step 2: Cutting sides

The sides are easily sawn to shape on a bandsaw or a with a sabre saw. Saw close to the lines and finish by sanding or by plane up to the line. Sanding can be many times more accurate than sawing.

Step 3: Bending the sides
Next we will bend the sides with a little water and heat. For this procedure we will be using a side bending jig that you can make. (See Section on Jigs) This jig is the exact shape of the sides and will yield very good results with a little practice. An alternate method of bending the sides is using a 4 inch metal pipe that is heated with a propane torch. (See Section on Jigs). We will using the side bending jig. See photos **5-2 and 5-3**.
See page **131**.

(**Photo 5-2**) Side view of the side bending jigs.

(**Photo 5-3**) An end view of the side bending jig

Step 4: Preparing the side bender

Without any water or heat practice aligning the waist line with the waist line mark on the side bender. Adjust the wooden cauls to accept the straight sides and align the heating blanket and the strait side of one side with the edge of the steel slat.

Step 5: Wetting and bending first side

Spray both sides with clean distilled water almost to the point of run-off. Prop the side on one end and allow excess water to run off of the side. Next, lay side flat on a clean surface and keep the wood damp by spraying only occasionally. Be ready to insert the side on the bender as you prepared. Plug in your silicone heating blanket and allow it to heat up for several minutes. You must work fast now and thing will be getting hot so wear gloves if you like. Tighten the waist caul evenly and almost all of the way down to the metal slat. Next bend the rear bout (end) the same way working the caul slowly towards the metal slat. Repeat the same for the forward bout.
Go back to each caul and tighten to the metal slat slowly. Do not add extra water while the wood is being bent, it might stain the wood. There are many opinions about how much water to use. See what work for you and your wood. Every

wood responds differently. Consider adding a rheostat to give you more choices to adjust the temperature and a timer for convenience.

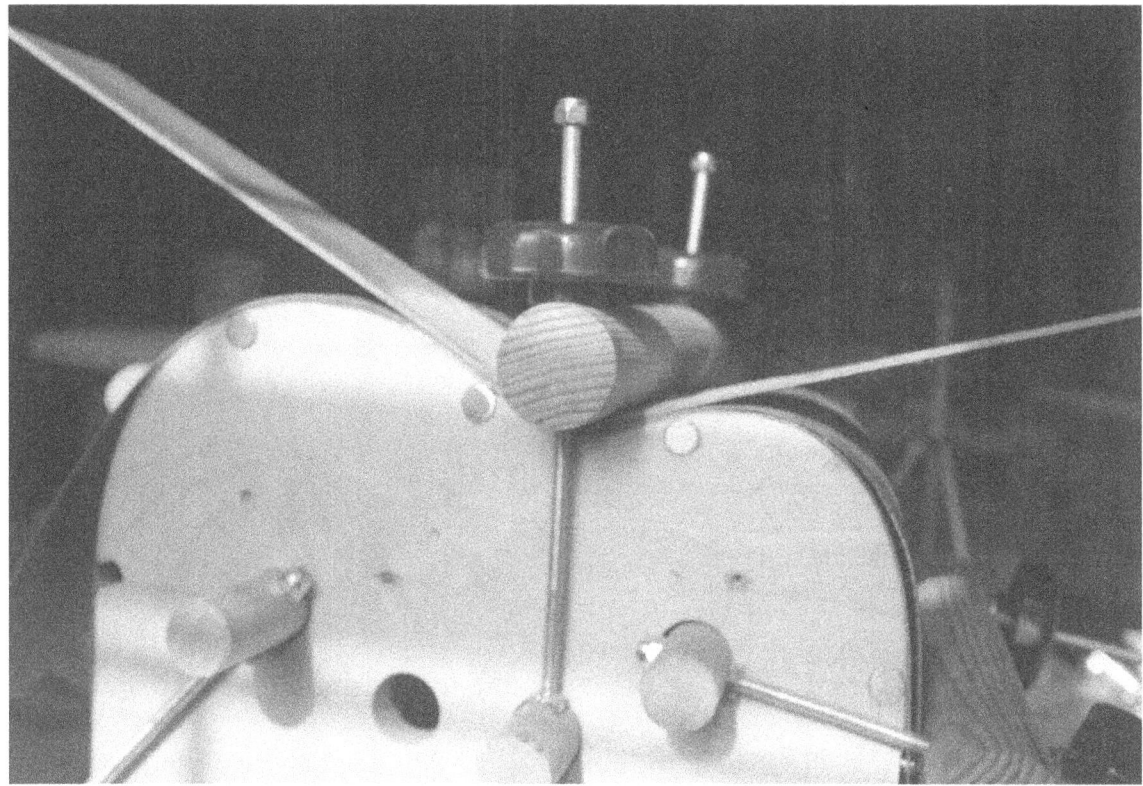

(**Photo 5-4**) The waist bout bent. The caul is tightened by the black knobs. By now the bending jig is very hot so work fast.

When bending the sides, steam will appear and at some point if the sides are heated too long, the steam will turn to smoke. Smoke is not good. You can begin to smell the difference and you should turn off the side bending jig and allow the sides to cool and stay in the jig for several hours.

Every type wood is different and will require a different heat exposure and different amounts of water and being kept wet for different lengths of time.

(**Photo 5-5**) Front and rear bouts bent. Heat in this position for 5 to 10 minutes

Allow the wood to cool while in the bending jig. Allow a couple of hours to let the wood cool to it's new form. Overnight is best. Once taken out of the jig it should be inserted into an assembly jig or mold. See section on *Jigs*.

Heat for the bending process with this technique is from a 600 watt silicone blanket. It produces even heat and can be used with a rheostat and a timer to adjust the temperature and time for various type of wood. The bending jig is a convenient and easy way to bend wood binding. Binding is bent the same way as the sides. You will get a perfect set of binding because the sides and binding are bent on the same profile. The heating time is less for bending the binding material. (See *Sources of Supplies* for heating blankets)

Bending sides with heated pipe.
An alternative method of bending the sides is to use a propane torch to heat a four inch diameter metal pipe 10 inches long. A baffle is wedged in the end of the pipe that faces you. It can be thin sheet metal bent over or tin and the end of the pipe must not be airtight. Different diameters of pipe are used for different parts of the sides. This method is somewhat difficult without some experience or in a classroom setting.

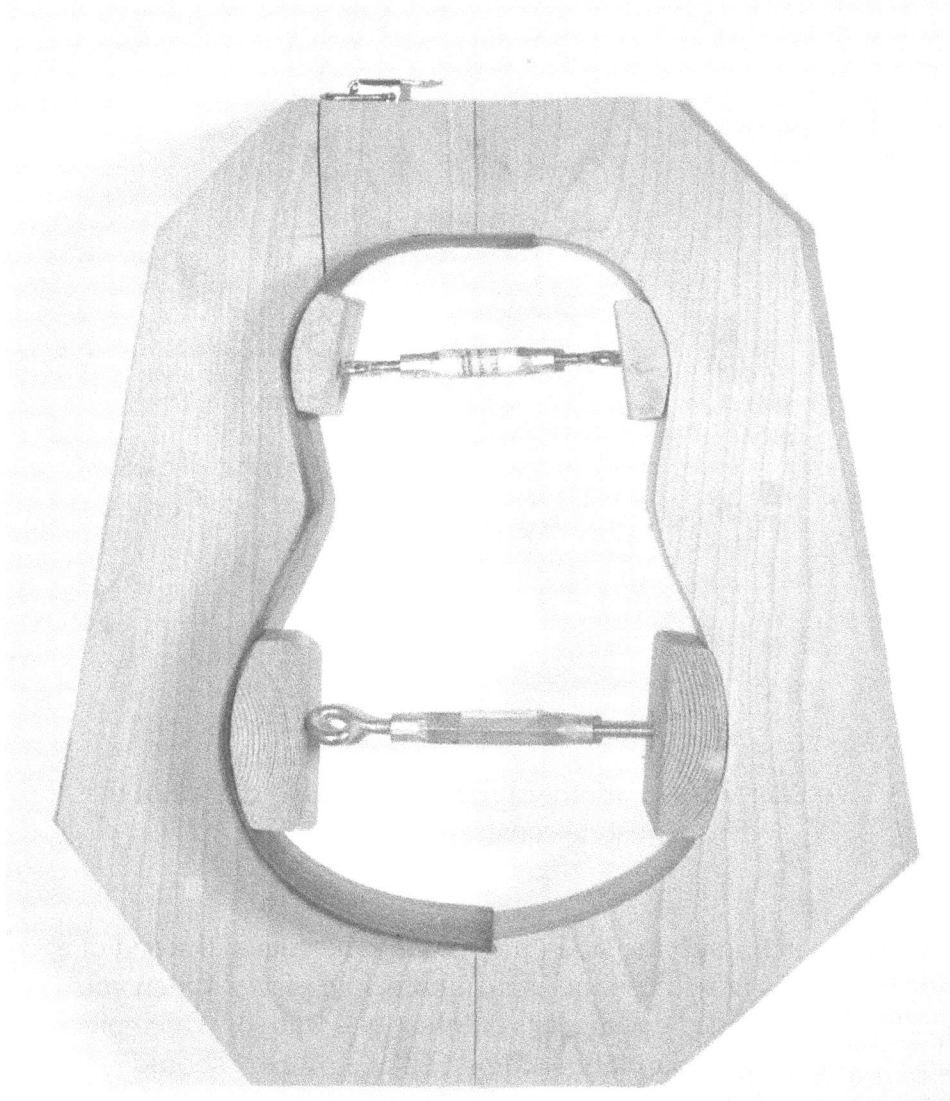

(**Photo 5-6**) First bent side clamped and stored in mold until other side is ready

Box Style Form

This mold is used for "Box Style" body construction and is used extensively during the entire soundbox construction process. The turn buckles and contoured cauls help to insure an accurate way to mark cut for trimming side to exact length. More on this mould in the *Assembly 1* section and section on *Jigs*. This method of construction is widely used in guitarmaking. This one is just smaller. The luggage latch is necessary to remove body from mold and to adjust body for the sanding process. The latch is released and the cut is spread apart with small screwdriver if necessary. Without this cut it would be very difficult to remove the body from the mold.

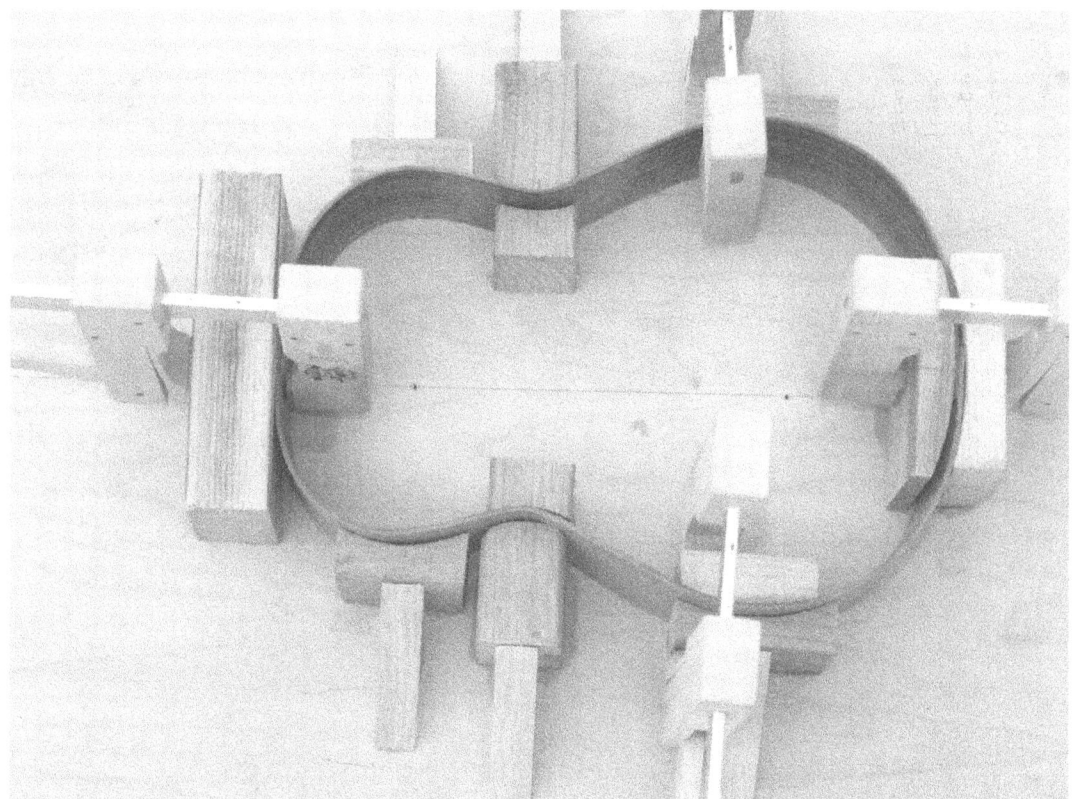

(**Photo 5-7**) Two bent sides in another type of assembly jig used in the Spanish style construction.

This jig is used to help in ling up the sides and making the cuts at the end of each side, front and back. This jig will used to glue tail block in place. When you remove each side from the side bending jig you must be aware of which piece is left and which is right. When you place a side on a flat surface it should lay flat. That is the top edge of that side. It is a good idea to mark each side until they are glued to the neck and tailblock.

End of Chapter 5

Please Notice

This book is intended to illustrate two methods of ukulele construction.

Box Style- This method involves building the soundbox and a neck as two separate units that will be joined together later in the construction process. This method gives free access completely around the body allowing one to install binding and purfling with ease. The neck has not been attached the time to rout the shelves for the binding.

Spanish Style- This approach to ukulele construction allows for the neck to be made as an integral part of the instrument. The sides are slid into saw kerf in the neck. This style ukulele is built in the same manor as a classical guitar. There is more work necessary to prepare the neck and some of the cuts must be exact.

Everything that we have learned so far in this book is identical for both methods of ukulele construction. Most of what is to come will be the same except for the steps in fabricating and attaching the necks. There are quirks in both methods that you must be deal with.

The next chapter will be concerned with the two different neck construction methods. Every attempt is made to keep the two methods as separate as much as possible. You will need to make a decision as to the style ukulele you would like to build. It would be extra work but you may consider building both methods. We built both ukuleles in this book using components similar to those found is ukulele building kits. We build both styles for the purpose of photographing the steps for this books.

Box Style

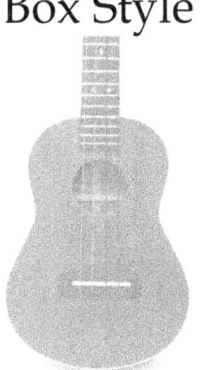

Spanish

Chapter 6

Necks

This chapter will explain the construction of a neck blank that is used for Box Style necks and Spanish Style necks. Each method will be demonstrated and differ only in several steps.

Most ukulele necks are made from quartersawn Honduran mahogany. It is a very stable wood and is somewhat resistant to environmental changes. It is easy to work with but is somewhat soft so care must be taken not to dent the wood. It is an open grain and pores need to be filled but it is capable of producing a flawless finish.

Other woods that make good necks are maple, koa, and Spanish cedar. Maple is harder and more difficult to carve and sand. It is a tight-grained wood that finishes well and is very resistant to wear. Maple can add new dimension to a ukulele using curly and birdseye maple. Koa and cedar a somewhat softer and it is more like mahogany in the way it works. Ukulele necks are not under great stress from the string and the fretboards are not subject to wear as with metal strings.

Procedure: Neck Blank Construction

Step 1: Choose tight grained quartersawn piece of mahogany 15/16 inch X 2 inch X 28 inches long. The two inch wide stock is not wide enough to make the headstock but it is acceptable practice to glue "ears" to the neck at the headstock. Two ¾ X 5/8 X 6 inch ears will be glued to each side of the headstock. Three inch wide wood can be used instead of gluing on the ears. You may have to adjust a dimension later in the construction. Plane and sand the neck blank to be flat and square. See cutting layout on the next page.

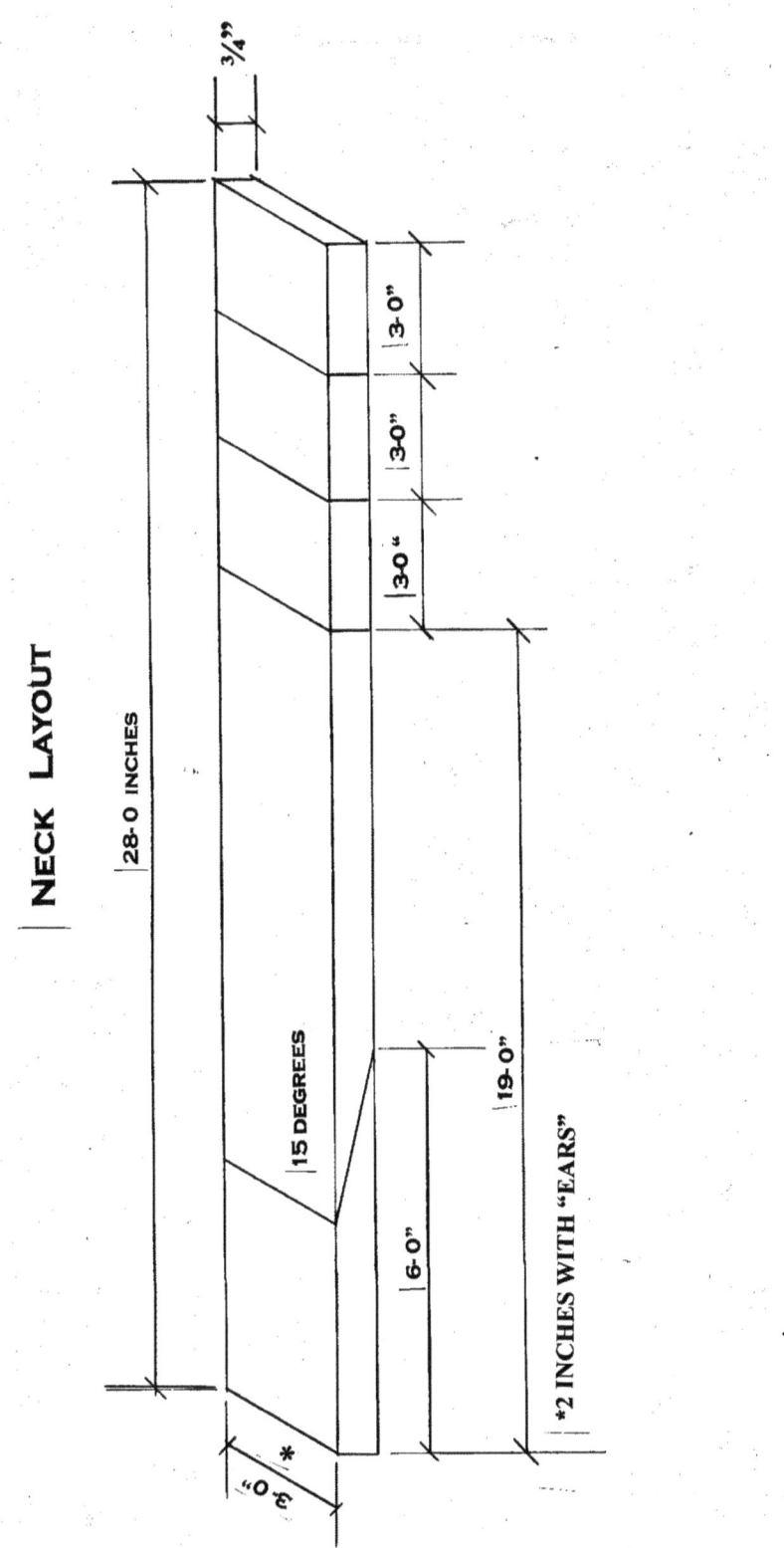

(Illustration 6-1) Cutting Layout for Neck

(**Photo 6-1**) Neck blank clamped to neck cutting jig. This jig allows you to cut a scarf joint at 15 degrees that is needed to build the neck. This jig is used for cutting and gluing the scarf joint.

(**Photo 6-2**) Cutting the headstock from neck blank

Step 2: Cut scarf joint.

This cut may be made on the band saw or table saw. The jig holds the neck blank safely during the cut. The headstock of the neck must be at this angle in order to exert downward pressure of the strings onto the nut. The cut is made 6 inches from one end.

Step 3: Sanding the joint

(**Photo 6-3**) Sanding one side of the neck blank that has been cut at a 15 degree angle. The 6 inch headstock piece will be glued to the bottom of the neck side of the neck blank.

(**Photo 6-4**) The headstock (small) part of the neck after being cut and sanded. The pencil line the middle of the wood was made with a square and was used as a guide while sanding the rough band saw cut. This will be the back of the 1/8 inch nut. The right side of the photo is the side that was cut and sanded and will produce a superior glue joint. The left side of the photo is the original part of the neck blank.

Step 4: Gluing headstock to neck

After the neck has been cut, sand both sides of the cut square in order to make a very strong glue joint. The cut on the smaller piece is the most important to keep the long cut square. You can tell how to sand by drawing a line perpendicular to the edge at the point where the cut meets the face of the long piece of the neck.

(Photo 6-5) Neck being glued using neck cutting and gluing jig. This jig help to glue the headstock to the neck at an accurate 15 degrees. Don't forget the wax paper !

Notice a small block of wood is clamped to the end of the jig. This helps the joint to keep from sliding apart. You will need to experiment with this operation.

While this part of the neck is drying, the heelblock can be glued together . There are three blocks that get glued to the other end of the neck. The three blocks can be glued as one procedure and then glued to the neck or all four pieces can be glued at one time. (see **Photo 6-6**) Gluing the heelblock in two procedures seems to allow for a neater job. The blocks move around when glue is applied and it is hard to line all of the blocks and neck together at one time. The location of the headblock is somewhat critical, especially for the Spanish style neck.

(**Photo 6-6**) Components of the he heelblock

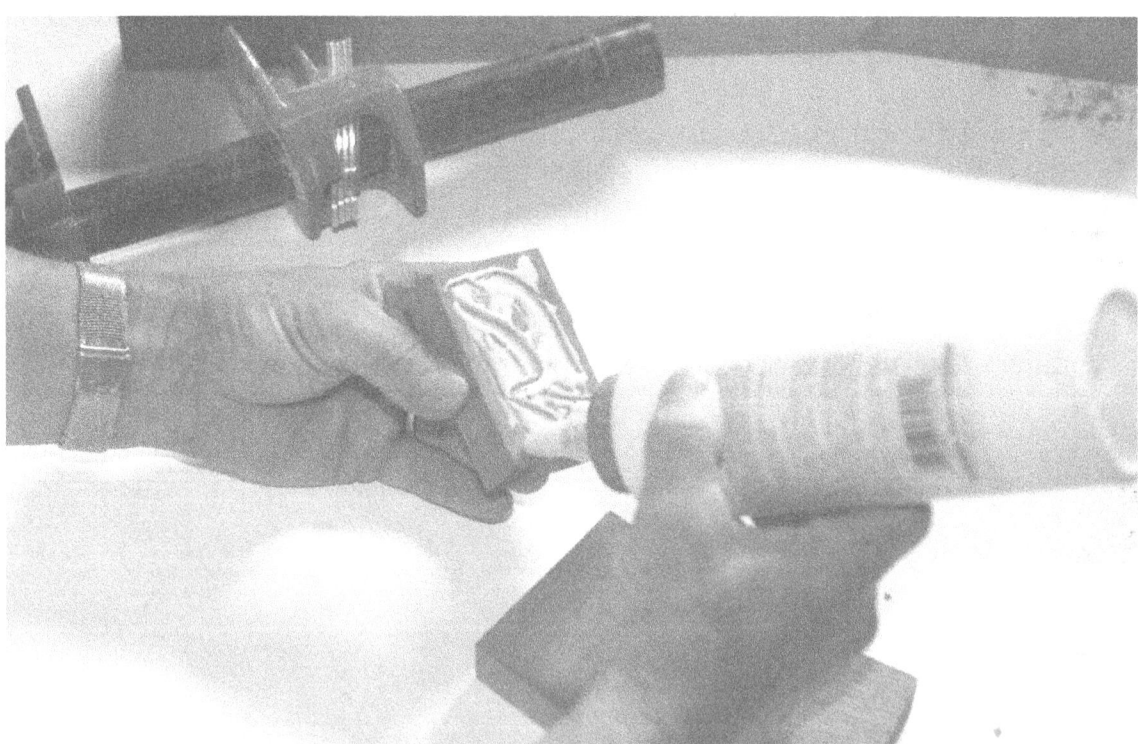

(**Photo 6-7**) Applying glue to heelblock components. Use enough glue to have a small amount squeeze out of the joints but not too much. When gluing these small blocks it is easy to apply glue to only one side and rub the joint together 5 or 6 times. That seems to help the glue begin to grab.

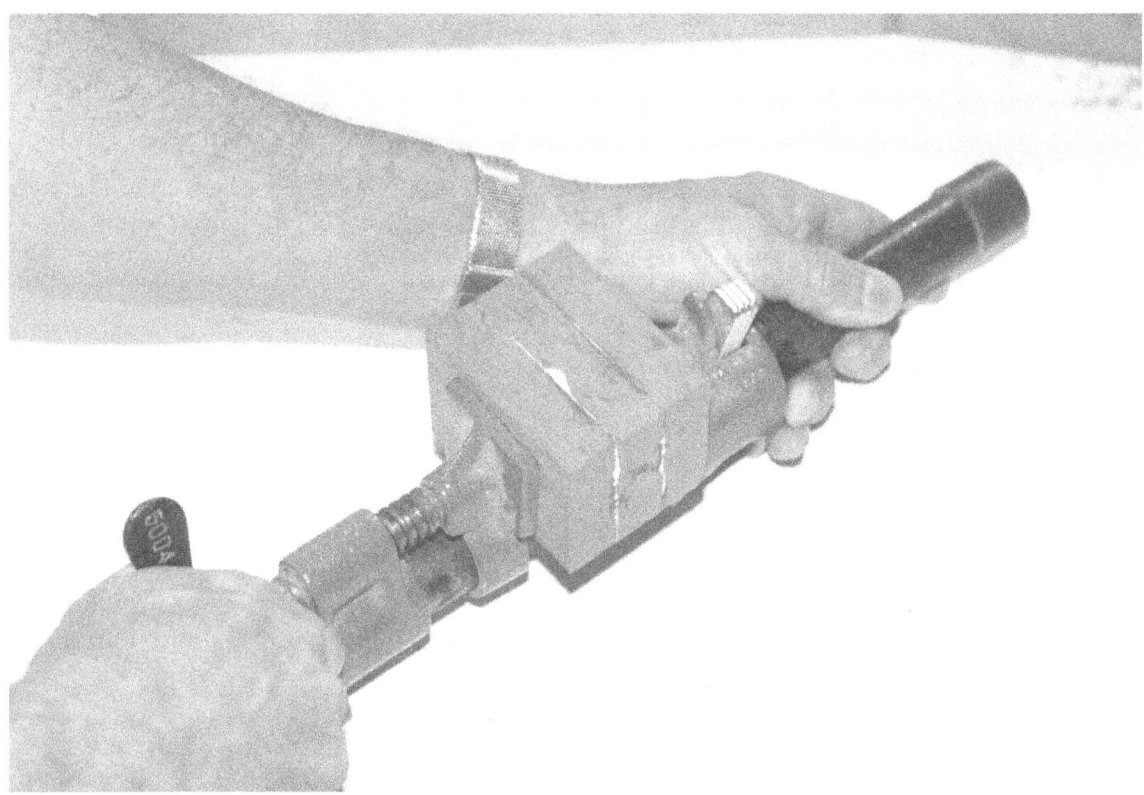

(**Photo 6-8**) The heelblock being clamped. Notice the small amount of glue being squeezed out of the joints, this is a good amount. Too much is not good.

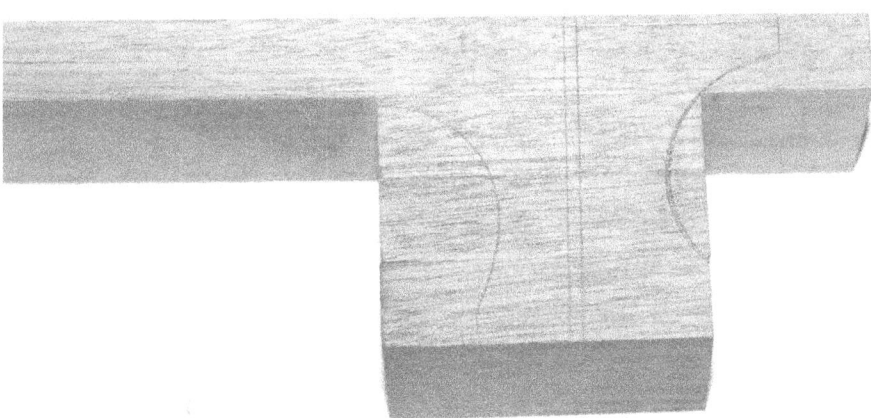

(**Photo 6-9**) The completed heelblock with the outline for a Spanish neck. The next step for this Spanish neck is to cut a groove in the neck at a slight angle to accept the sides. For a Box Style neck the head block will be cut all of the way thru at the same place as the grooves are to be cut.(See **Photo 6-10**)

Step 5: Neck Layout

The neck will join the body at the 14th fret. Mark a centerline on all components and mark two lines 1/8 inch apart at the point where the neck meets the headstock. (See **Photo 6-11**) This is where the nut will be located and the length of the neck and scale will start here. Be accurate with this measurement. The top of the neck tapers from 1- 3/8 inch at the nut to 1-3/4 where the sides meet the neck slots, at the 14th fret.

Step 6: Spanish Neck

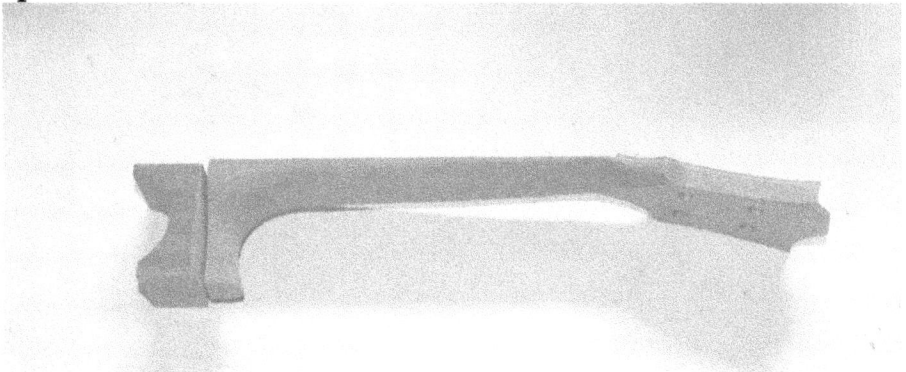

(**Photo 6-10**)   Example of a Spanish style neck

(**Photo 6-11**) Using the sliding table jig on the table saw, cut right slot to receive sides at 1 ½ degrees angled towards the body end of the neck. See section on *Jigs* . These cut must be made with a **thin kerf** blade because a regular saw blade has a 1/8 inch kerf which is too wide for the side material. The sliding table jig is used for these cuts. (See section on *Jigs*)

(**Photo 6-12**) Same cut on left side of neck. Notice wooden block to hold heel away from the sliding table jig to keep the neck parallel. Be sure to have the two cuts line up perfectly because the sides will be inserted in these grooves. You must keep the neck and body straight along the centerline.

These two cut may also be cut on a radial arm saw. The cut are at 1 ½ degrees and cut into neck blank and leave approximately ½ inch of wood where the two cuts would meet. You will need to adjust this depth with different neck wood widths. If you have a radial arm saw, this is the better way to cut these grooves.

Step 6: Cutting excess wood from heel with sliding table on table saw used as *wood nibbler jig*. Start cutting wood away at the 1 ½ degree angle cut made in **Photos 6-11 and 6-12**. Cut away wood away from the body side of the angle cut only. Set up the *neck nibbler* will require some trial and error cuts. Once you have a proper setting, make notes: height of blade, width of neck blank, traveling distance before stop block.

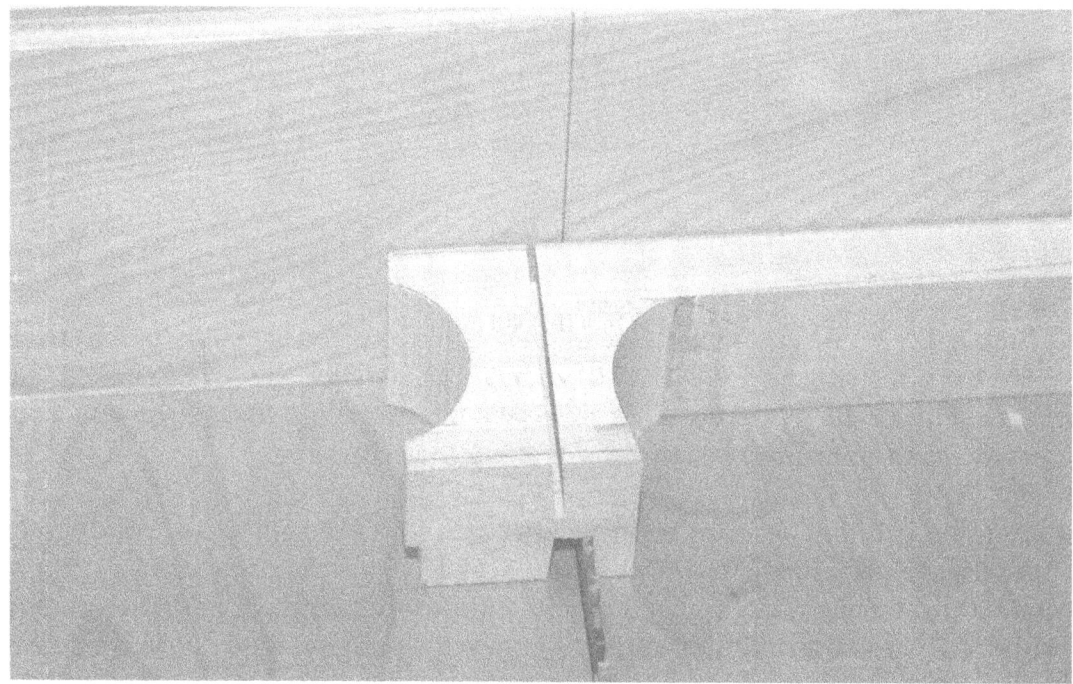

(**Photo 6-13**) Using sliding table jig on table saw to cut away excess wood in the heel area. Do this on both sides of neck. This is known a the "neck nibbler" and can be a real time saver and it is worth the time need to set up jig.

After this procedure, the tapers of the neck is measured and drawn on the top of the neck, where the fretboard will be attached and the side profile. Cut as many cuts that need to be square before cutting the top taper.

(Photo 6-14)   Cutting the taper on the edge of the neck.

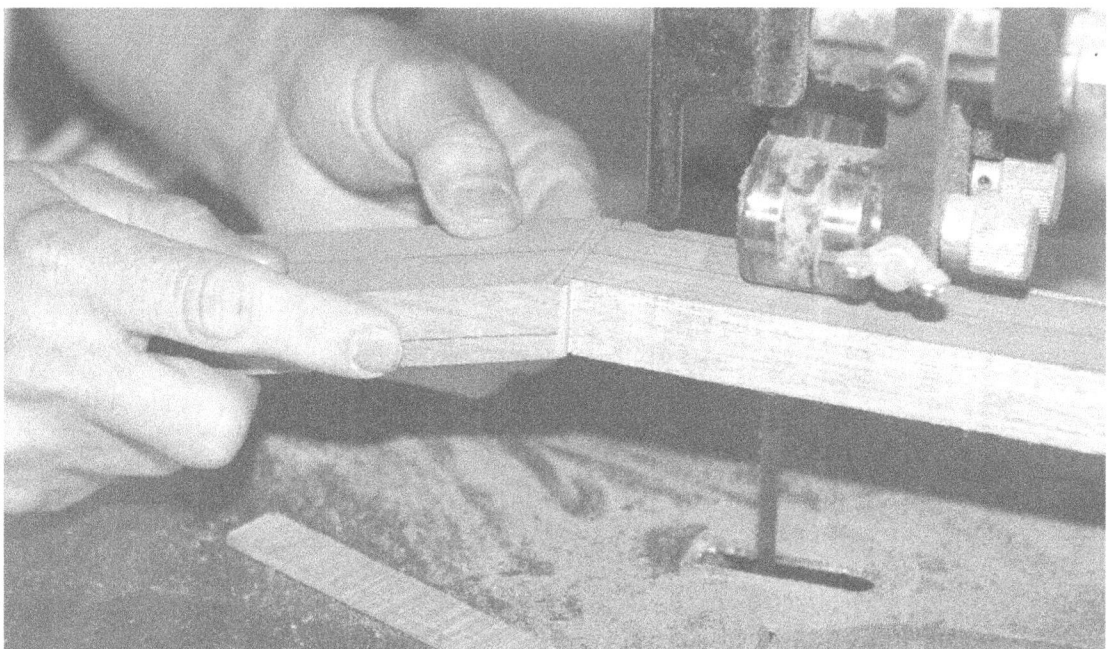

(Photo 6-15) Cutting the taper in the top of the neck. Do not cut closer that 1/16+ to the line to allow room for error when the fretboard is attached.

(**Photo 6-16**) Cutting the "shelf" for the top to fit flush with the bottom of the fretboard when the soundboard it attached. The depth of this cut is the same as the thickness of the top. Wait to make this cut until you have the thickness of the prepared soundboard. This cut extends to the slots that were made to accept the sides. This cut is necessarily only with the Spanish style neck.

(**Photo 6-17**) Notice the curved saw kerfs that were made with the sliding table on the table saw. (See Sliding Table Saw Jig in the *Jig* section *Neck Nibbler*) Always file towards the centerline to prevent splits near neck's edge. The saw will need to be adjusted to leave approximately 3/8 inch on the top of the neck where the fretboard will be and about 1 wide inch at the heel. This cut is curve similar to the shape of the finished heel. This step will save time carving and rasping. his step is optional if you want to carve the heel.

To carve the heel, use left and right flex chisels and curved chisel. You can finish the rough cuts with files and a riffler. It may take a little longer but you do not have to spend so much time setting up the nibbler jig. If you are making only one instrument carving might be a good alternative.

Step 7: Rough carving neck

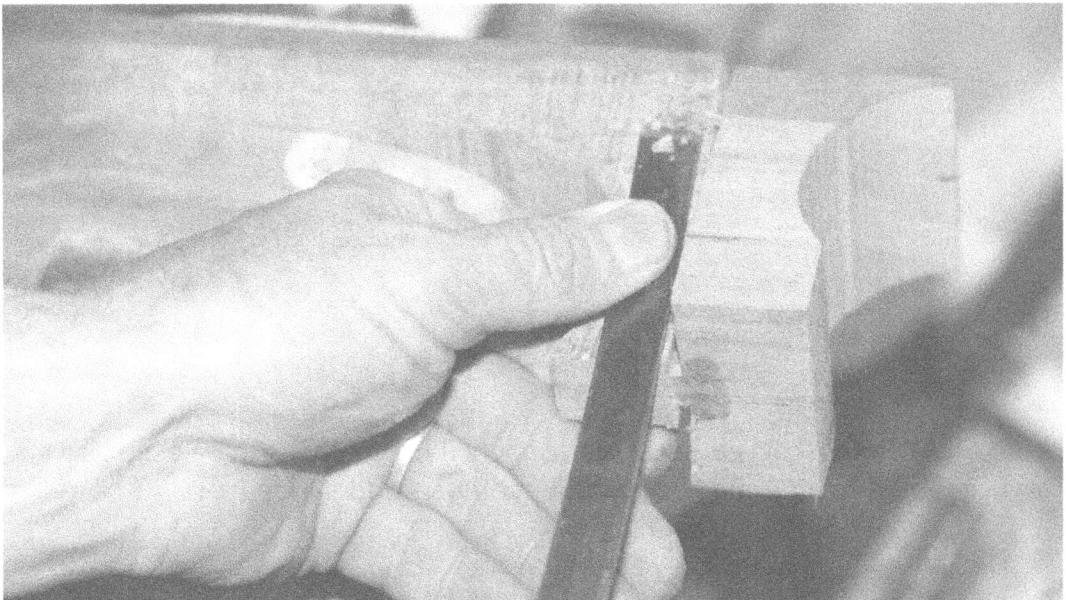

(**Photo 6-18**) Carving ramp of heel with curved chisel where the neck nibbler has remove most of the wood. Use caution when cutting towards the edge of the neck blank. Here the neck nibbler has done most of the work and this cut is only smoothing the saw blade marks.

(**Photo 6-19**)　　　Carving heel with a flex gouge

(Photo 6-20) Rough carved heel. Notice pencil line on neck to be used as a reference while shaping the neck profile with files and sandpaper.

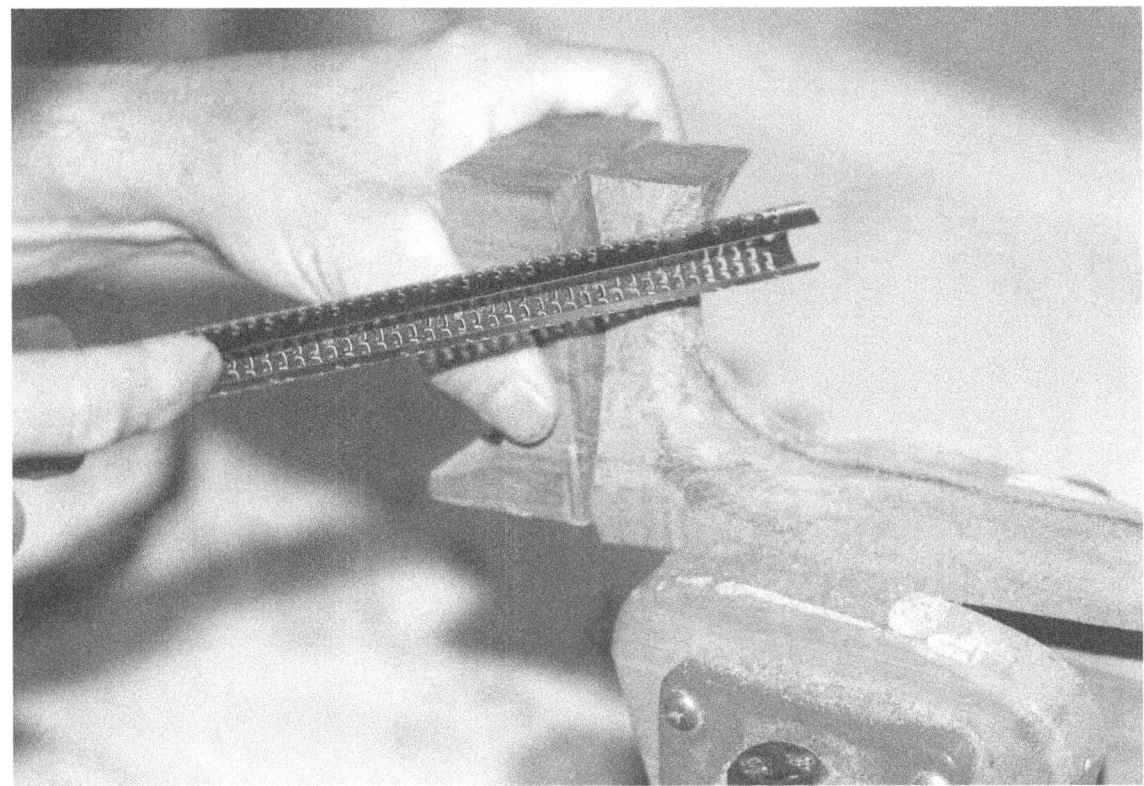

(**Photo 6-21**) Refining heel of Spanish style neck with round Micro Plane

(**Photo 6-22**) Maintain and use a centerline on the neck to help create an even neck.

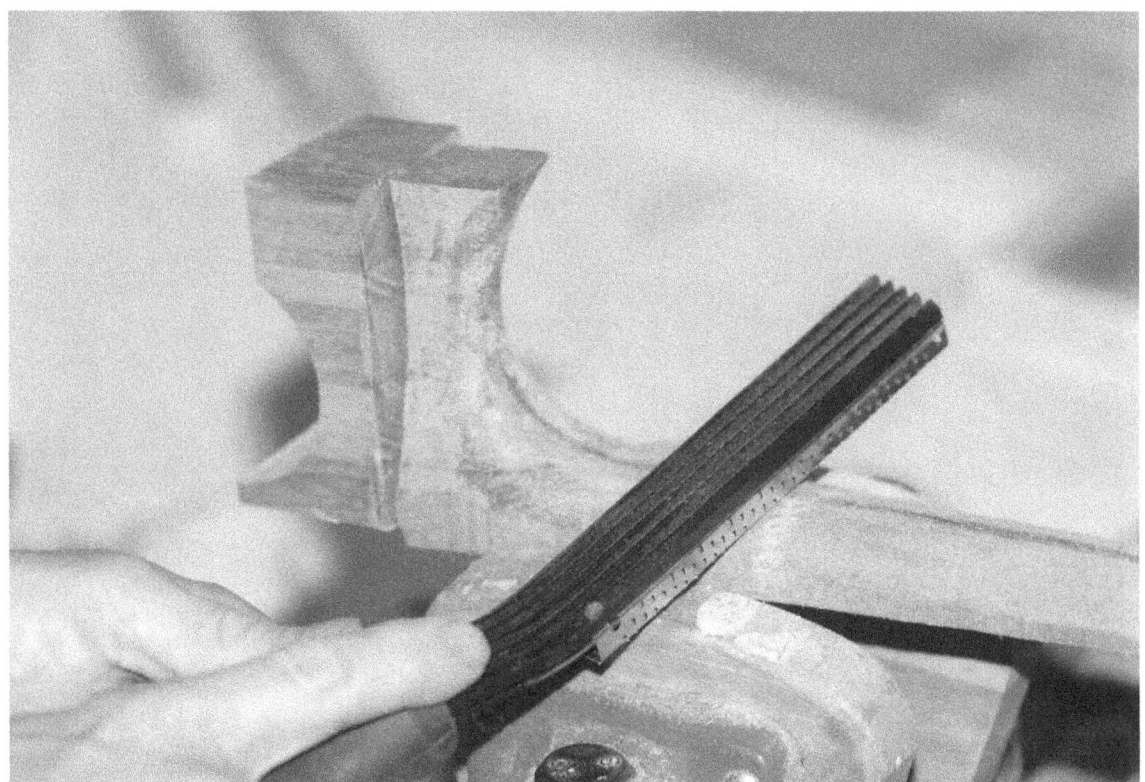

(Photo 6-23) Working on neck with micro plane

(Photo 6-24) A wood rasp shaping the heel area of a Spanish style neck.

(**Photo 6-25**) The beginning of the neck sanding process. Start with 120 grit paper and work to 400 grit paper..

(**Photo 6-26**) Shaping the neck at the transition from the neck to headplate

Step 8: Box Style Neck

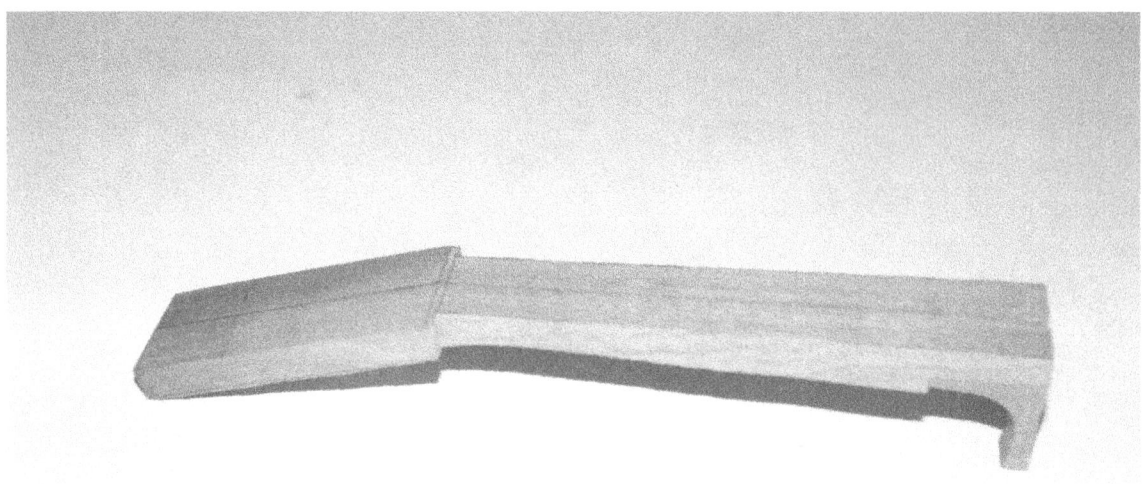

(Photo 6-27) Example of a rough neck for Box type construction

The Box Style neck is the same as the Spanish Style neck except that is does not extend into the soundbox. The soundbox and the neck are two separate components that are joined together after each piece is built. The two pieces are held together by a sliding dovetail joint, a mortise and tenon joint, spline or biscuit inserted into a slot or a bolt-on neck.

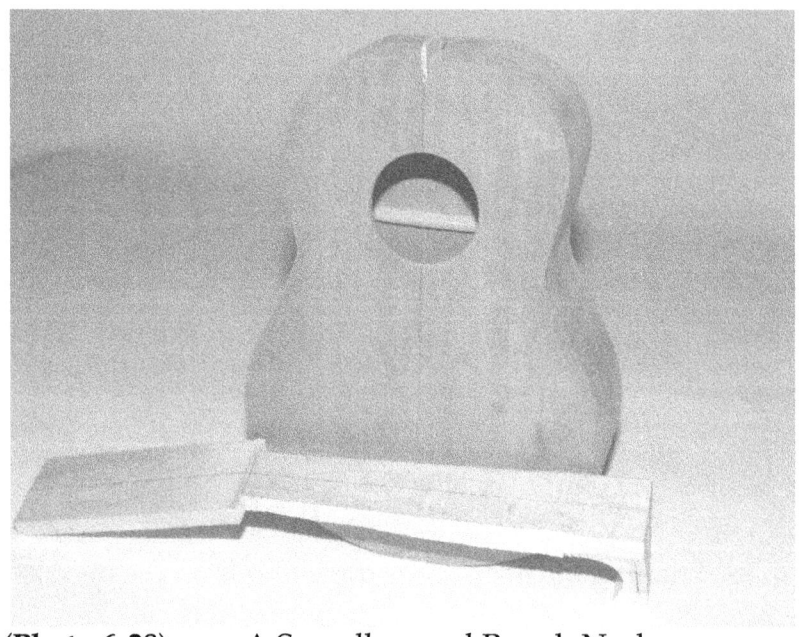

(Photo 6-28) A Soundbox and Rough Neck

(**Photo 6-25**) The beginning of the neck sanding process. Start with 120 grit paper and work to 400 grit paper..

(**Photo 6-26**) Shaping the neck at the transition from the neck to headplate

Step 8: Box Style Neck

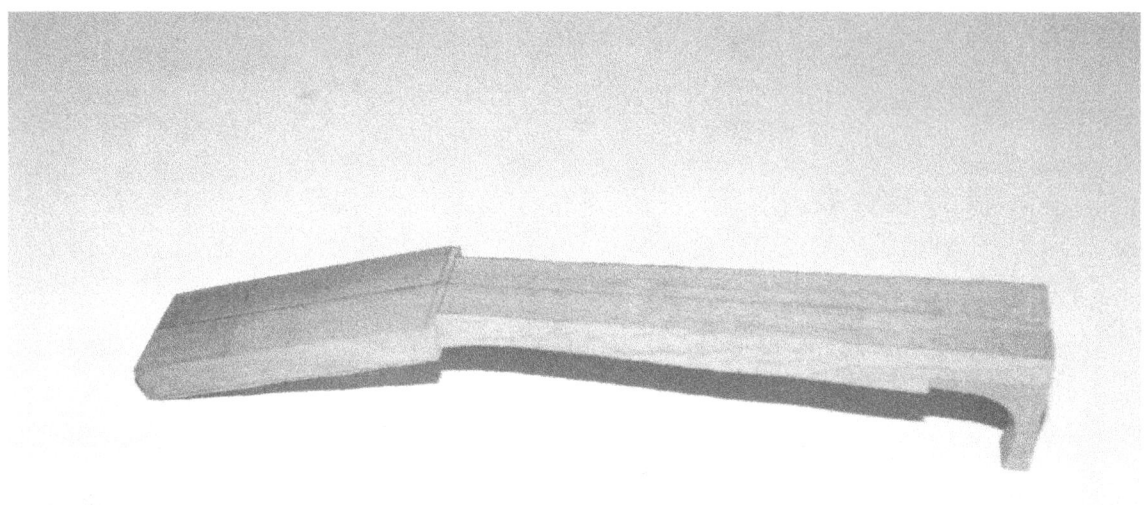

(Photo 6-27)   Example of a rough neck for Box type construction

The Box Style neck is the same as the Spanish Style neck except that is does not extend into the soundbox. The soundbox and the neck are two separate components that are joined together after each piece is built. The two pieces are held together by a sliding dovetail joint, a mortise and tenon joint, spline or biscuit inserted into a slot or a bolt-on neck.

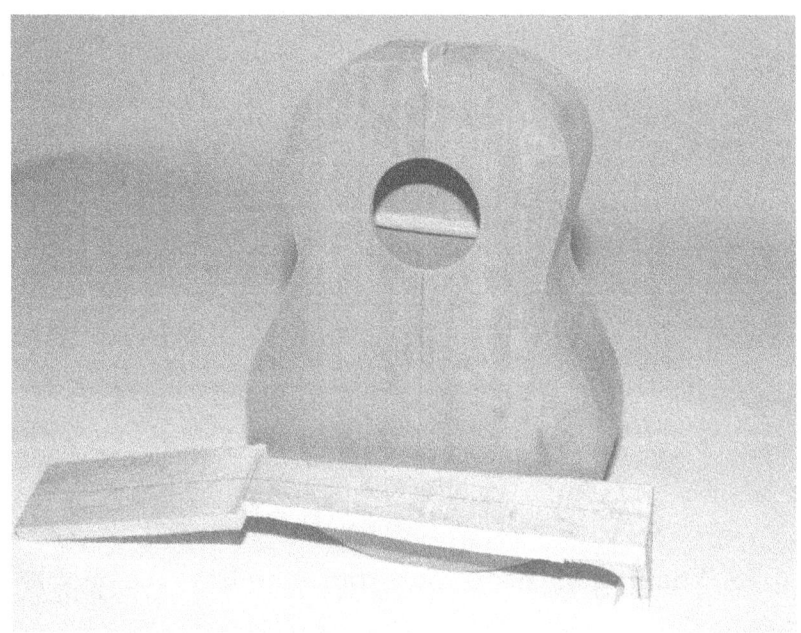

(Photo 6-28)   A Soundbox and Rough Neck

(Photo 6-29) Biscuit fitted into slot cut on sliding table jig on table saw. The slot is cut with the soundbox clamped on the back side of our sliding table jig. The top of the instrument is flat so the cut can be perfect. Be very accurate on this cut. Notice the flat area where neck is attached to the body. This is very important.

(Photo 6-30) Cutting slot for biscuit. Confirm setup for this important cut

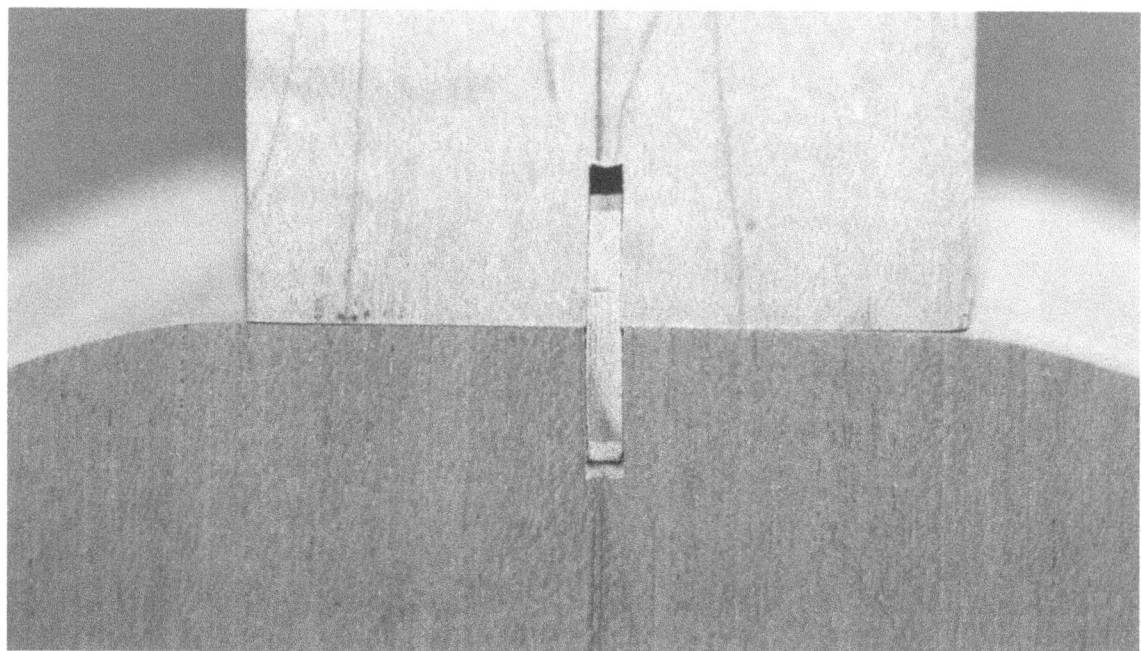

(Photo 6-32) Soundbox and neck joined by biscuit in grooves

This joint does not rely on the beech biscuit for strength, it is for alignment. The neck is glued to the body with epoxy and the extended fretboard is glued to the soundboard with titebond glue. Titebond glue can be used to glue the neck to the body also. Some think that the end grain will not make a strong bond.

The grooves for the biscuit is only 3/4 inch deep into the neck and the body. The beech biscuit are formed under great pressure and when the moisture in the glue comes into contact with the biscuit it swells. It forms a very tight fit. This slot is best cut with 1/8 inch saw blade.

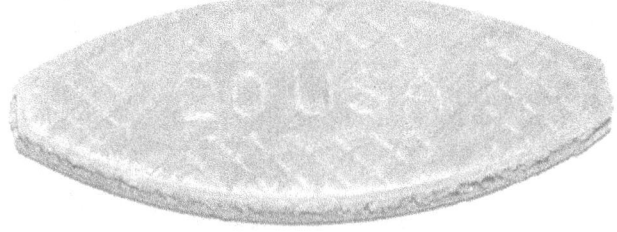

(Photo 6-33) A beech biscuit stamped under great pressure that will expand when glue is applied to form an amazing union. It is perfect to help an end grain joint.

(Photo 6-34) Shaping the heel of Box style neck. Notice it is much easier to work on the neck without the headblock in the way. The biscuit can be seen just below wood rasp.

(Photo 6-35) If you are using a neck blank less than 3 inches it will be necessary to glue on headblock extensions. The "ears" are glued on after all milling and rough carving is finished. They are small mahogany blocks 3/4 x 5/8 x 6 inches. They extend the headpiece to allow for a larger headpiece. The ears will be sanded flush with the top to accept the headpeice veneer.

Step 9: Headstock Veneer

The headpiece veneer is used to cover up the scarf joint and it lends some strength to the headpiece. When stacking several pieces of veneer it will help to pin them in place so they do not move around when the gluing process begins. This is a chance to add a subtle decoration to your instrument. Usually the headstock veneer is a fancy or particularly beautiful piece of veneer that might match the fretboard and bridge.

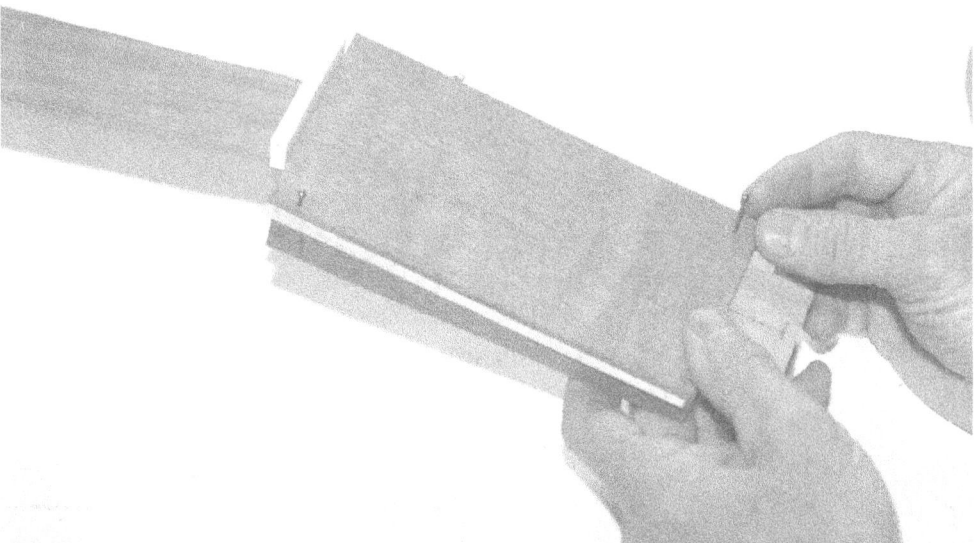

(**Photo 6-36**) Arranging veneer on headstock for gluing. Small pins help to keep layers straight while gluing. Locate the nut position and stick with double stick tape to help align the headstock veneer.

(**Photo 6-37**) Headstock veneer glued and clamped with four clamps and clamping caul.

(**Photo 6-38**) Headstock being sawn to shape. Notice the thin maple veneer sandwiched between headplate and top veneer. The headstock must be raised to a level to make the bandsaw cuts square to the top.

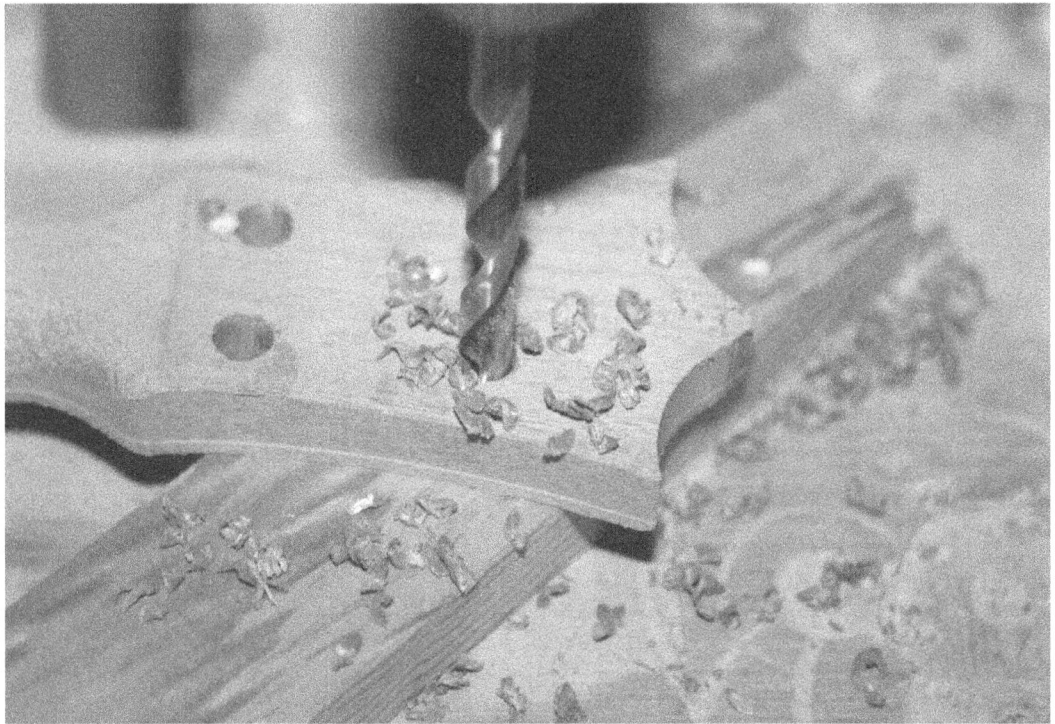

(**Photo 6-39**) Drilling 10 mm holes for tuning machines. Confirm size the size of your tuning machines before drilling holes.

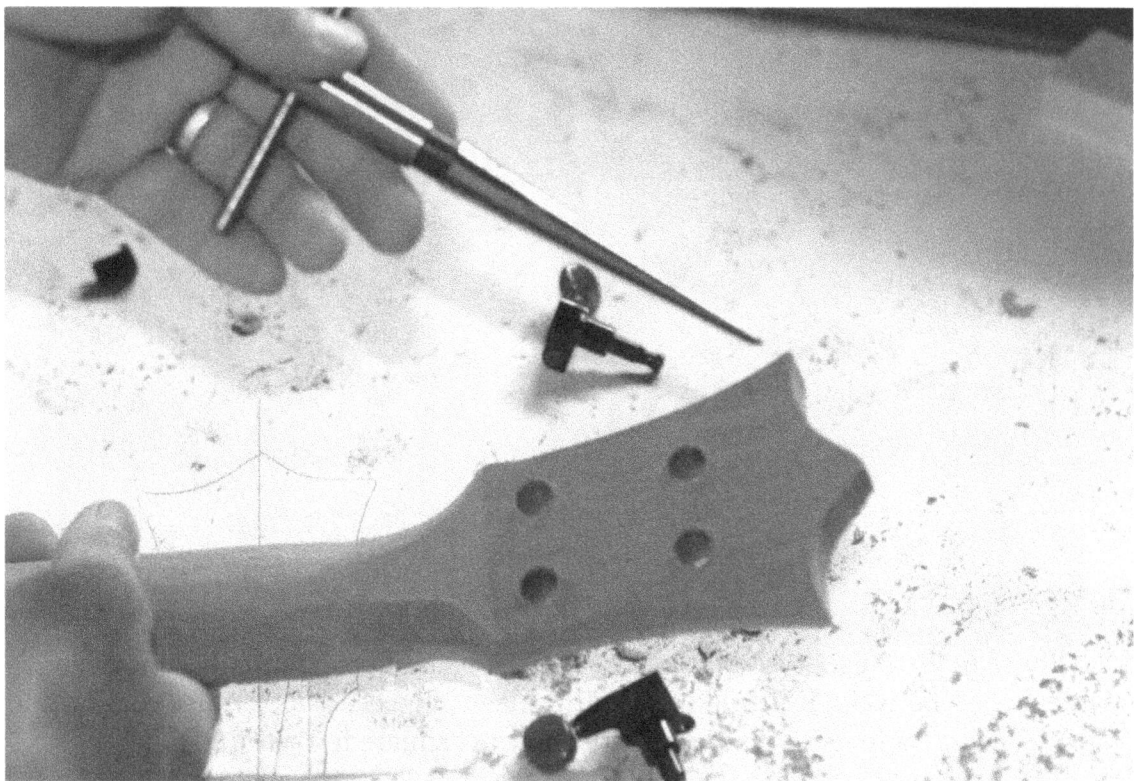

(Photo 6-40) If tuning machines fit tight in 10mm hole, ream to fit. Check size often to avoid making a hole that is too large.

End of Chapter 6

Chapter 7
Fretboard

Procedure: Layout of fretboard and installing frets

Step 1: Lay out shape of fretboard

The fretboard should be surfaced all four sides, true and square. The thickness should be 3/16 inch to 1/4 inch. Make sure the two long sides are parallel. Draw a centerline on the front, back and the ends. Finished size of the fretboard is 1-3/8 inch wide at the nut and 1-3/4 at the 14th fret and the taper should continue to the 20th fret. Not all of the frets slots will be used but continue your marks. After the fret slots are cut, cut the fretboard taper to 1/16+ inch on the outside of the lines like on the neck. This extra width will be filed off later along with the neck.

If you can determine how many frets you will be using, you can stop cutting the fret slots and make an interesting design at the end of the fretboard at the soundhole.

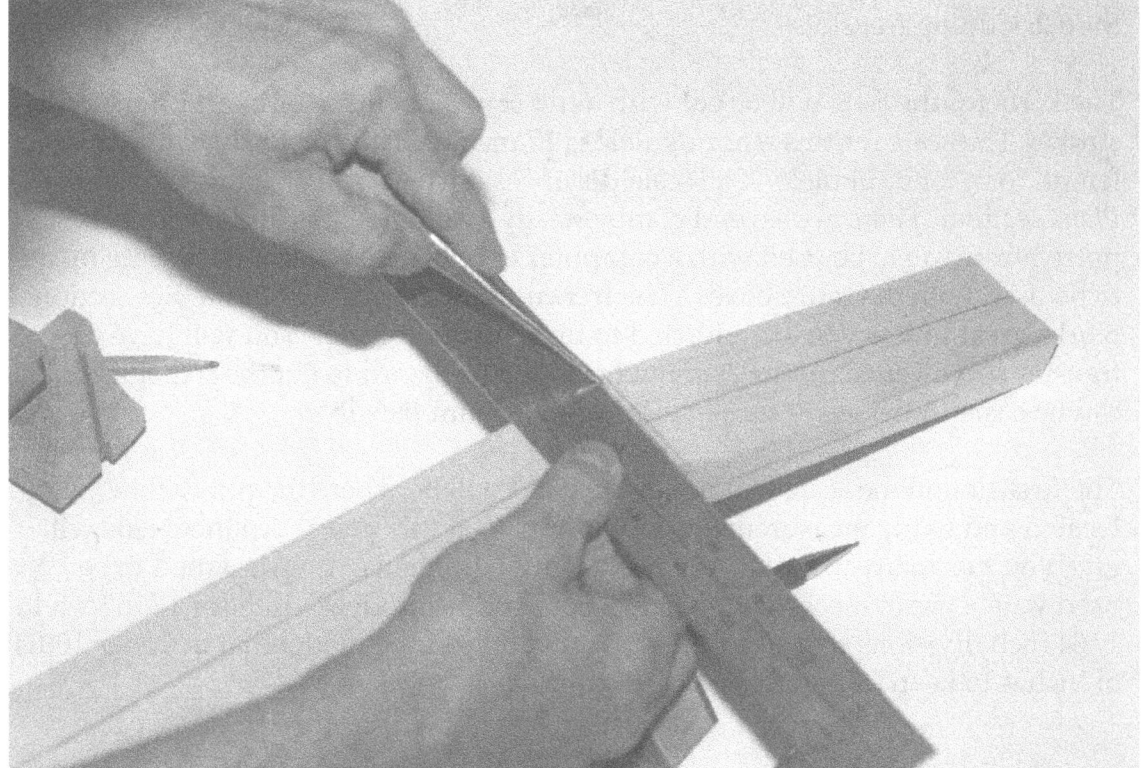

(**Photo 7-1**) Mark centerline on all sides. This is best done with a center finding ruler. Use an awl to make marks in the wood for later reference. The marks in the wood will be covered by fretboard and headplate.

(**Photo 7-2**)   Scribing line with a marking knife to mark finish profile.

Step 2: Cutting fret slots

The kerfs for the frets will be cut with a fret saw that cuts a .024 kerf on the pull stroke. The scale for this tenor ukulele is 17 inches. This is a fairly common scale length for a tenor ukulele. The scale distances are listed on a chart in the *Jigs & Plans* section. There are several commercially available saws and a very nice mitre box made to be used with a computer cut plexiglas fretting template made to be used with the mitre boxes. The fret cutting jig described in the *Jigs* section works great unless you are addicted to tools, then buy one. You will have to transfer some very exact measurements to the fretboard to cut the fret slots but it can be easier done using an Incra Rule and a .5mm pencil.

The first slot on the scale will be cut thru and will be where the nut will be located and many measurements will originate at this point. An Incra rule will give you the ability to make very precise measurements. It is designed to be used with a .5mm mechanical pencil. Some of the models will have 1/16 inch to 1/64 inch divisions as well as 10ths. You will need the model that includes 10ths of inches to keep from having a math trauma.

(Photo 7-3) Fret Slot Cutting Jig

This is a fret saw that cuts on the pull stroke and has a blade width of .024 inches. There is a brass back on the saw that will allow you to cut only to the depth as determined by the height of the guide block. This depth can be adjusted by gluing thin strips of veneer on top of the glide block.

(Photo 7-4) A different view of the same setup.

(7-5)   Commercial mitre box with plexiglas fretting template

The fret cutting template is taped to the bottom side of the fretboard with carpet tape or double sided tape. The template has each fret position slotted to mate with a small pin on the mitre box. The fretboard can be cut with pinpoint accuracy in about ten minutes. Some luthier supply houses offer slotting fretboards to a 17 inch scale. If you just want to buy the template you can modify the simple jig as in photo 7-3. A fret scale calculation chart can be found in the *Plans* section. The fretboard on ukuleles are flat. That is, they do not have a radius sanded into the like many other stringed instruments. For example, many guitars have a 16 inch radius sanded into the fretboards.

(Photo 7-6)   A close-up view of the fret slotting template

Step 3: Drilling holes for fretboard markers

Before the frets are installed the fretboard markers are marked and drilled on the drill press. The markers are on the centerline exactly between the frets at 3,5,7,9, and 10th fret. Fretboard markers are optional but most ukuleles have this embellishment. They are usually 4mm or 5mm dots of mop or paua shell.

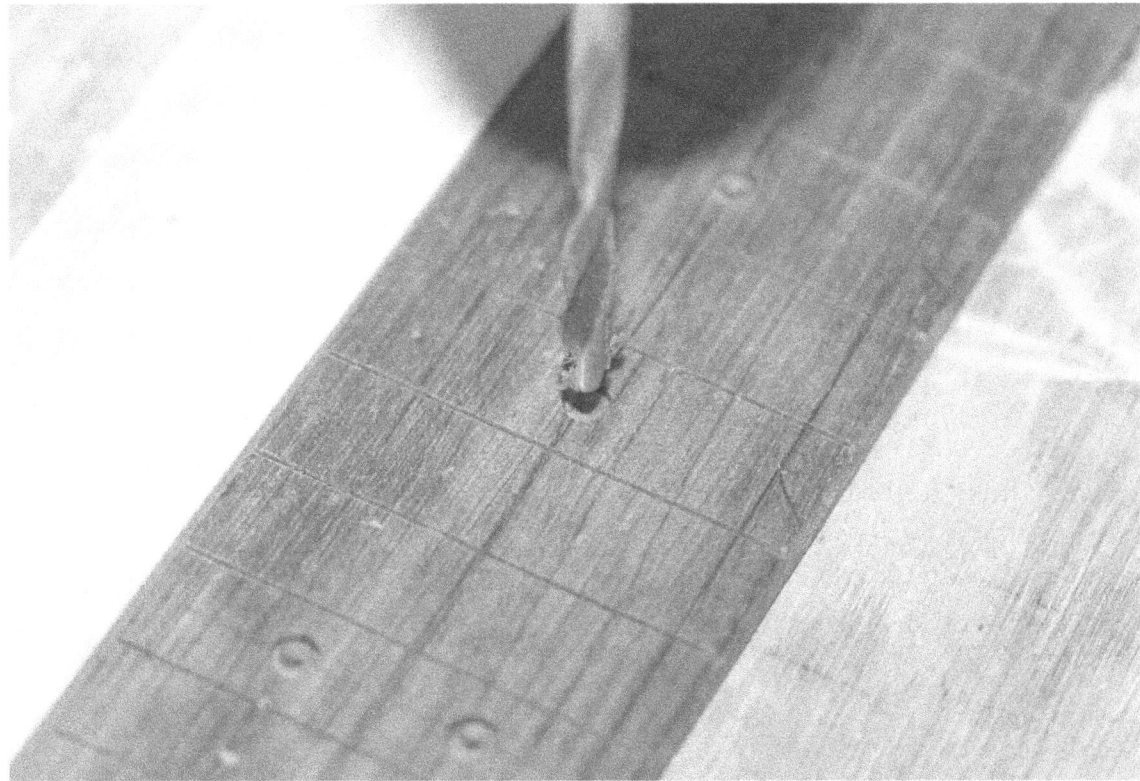

(Photo 7-7)   Fretboard being drilled for shell markers

Step 4: Fretboard cut to tapered outline

The step before gluing marker dots, is the fretboard is cut to size about 1/16 inch outside the line marked earlier. It will be filed and sanded to exact size once the frets are installed. This method allows for the fret to be installed before the fretboard is glued to the neck. After the fretboard is edge sanded, the side marker dots are installed corresponding to the marker dot on the fretboard, if desired. The side marker dots are usually 1/16 inch or 3/32 inch plastic rods that are cut flush after being glued in place. 2mm mop and paua dots are readily available also.

(Photo 7-8) Fretboard being cut to taper on bandsaw

Step 5: Inlay fretboard markers

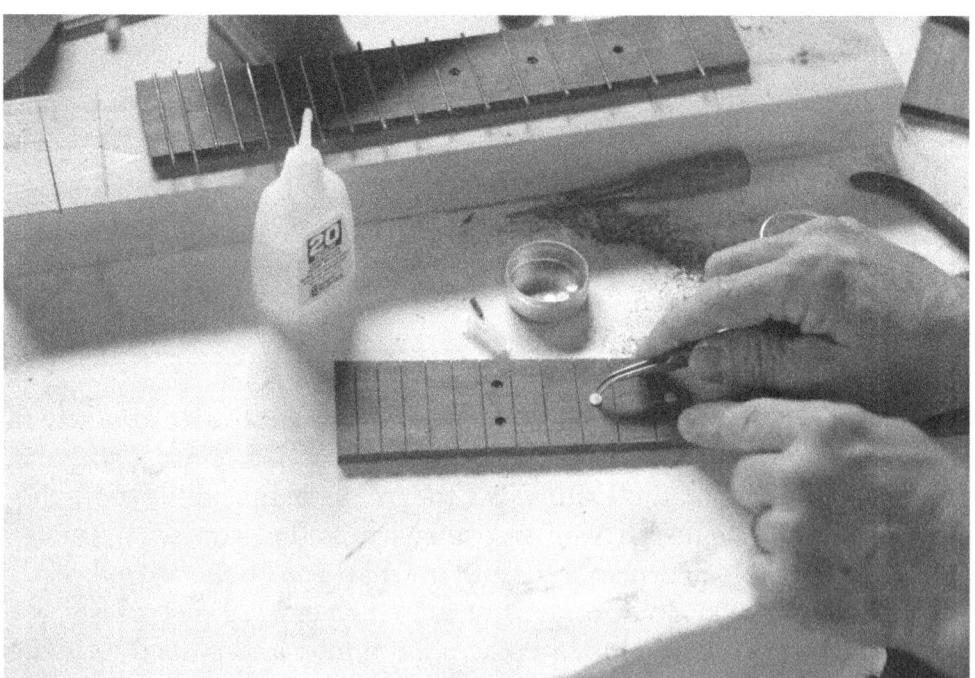

(Photo 7-9) Mother of Pearl dot being glued into holes drilled in fretboard with Cyano glue

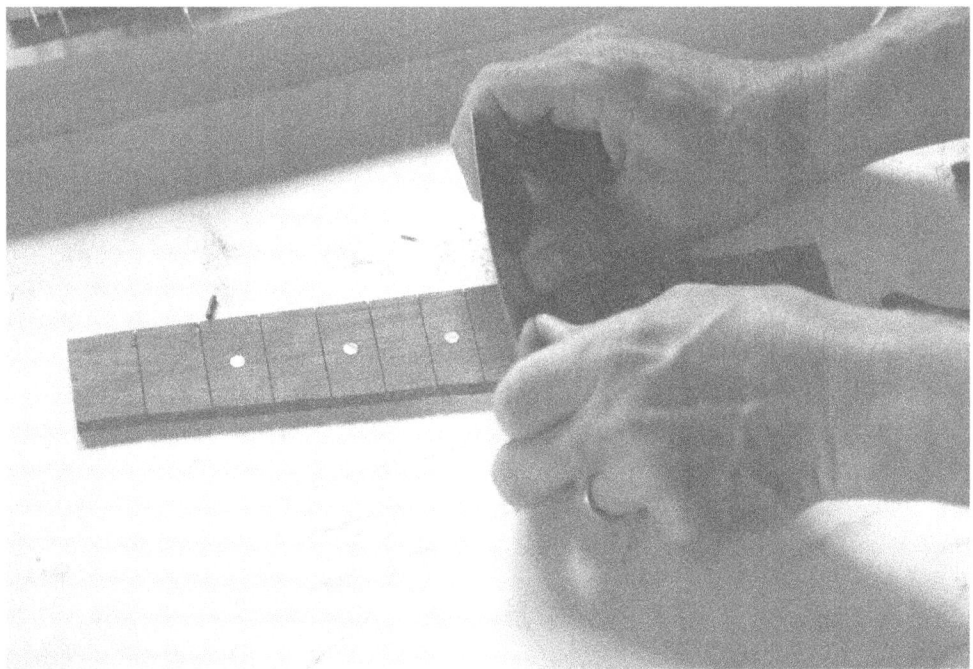

(**Photo 7-10**) Using scraper to level MOP dots on fretboard when dry

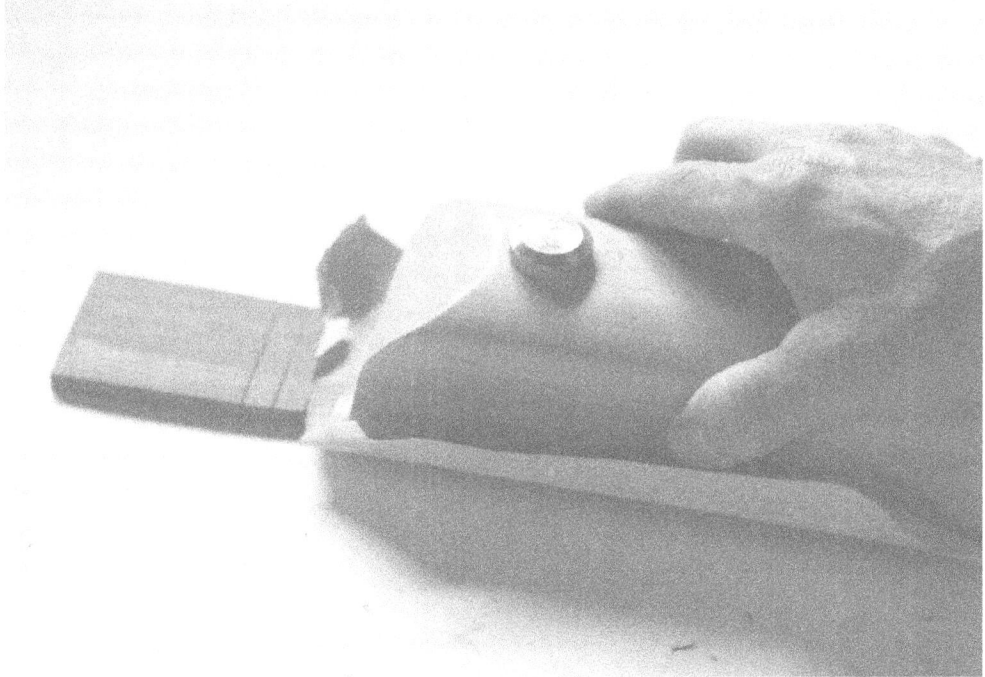

(**Photo 7-11**) This is the last chance to sand fretboard before frets are installed. Sand progressively down to 320 grit. This is the last time for any sanding on the fretboard because of the frets. Use a long sanding block that will insure a dead level fretboard.

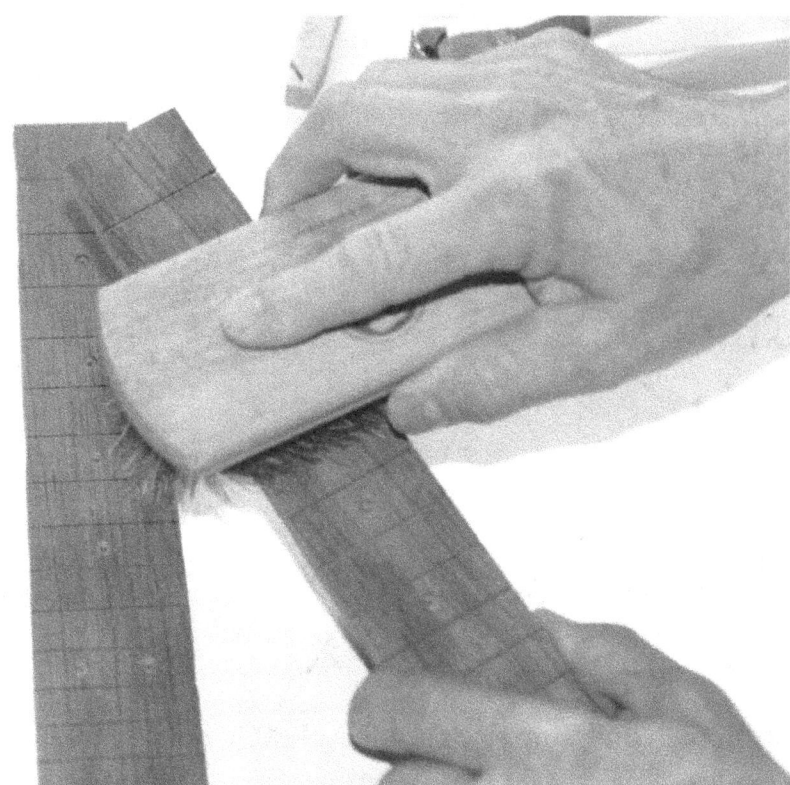

(**Photo 7-12**) Clean fret slots thoroughly with bristle brush

Step 6: Installing frets

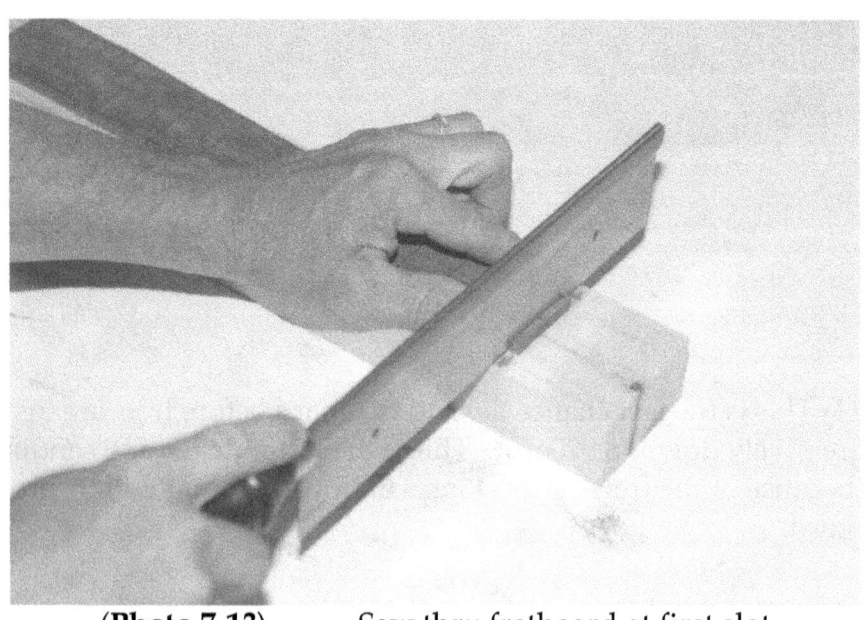

(**Photo 7-13**)   Saw thru fretboard at first slot

The fretwire that we will use is SM #0147 and it is supplied in straight 2 foot long lengths. Cut 16 pieces of #147 nickel-silver fretwire 2 1/4 inches long. Start the fretting process by gently tapping a piece of fretwire into the first fret slot on the far side of the fretboard. Hammer the fretwire into the slot across the fretboard using a nylon or brass faced hammer. Hold the fretwire close to the top of the fretboard and gently hammer. Confirm that the fret is seated straight and that the tang is near the bottom of the fret slot, about 1/32 inch.

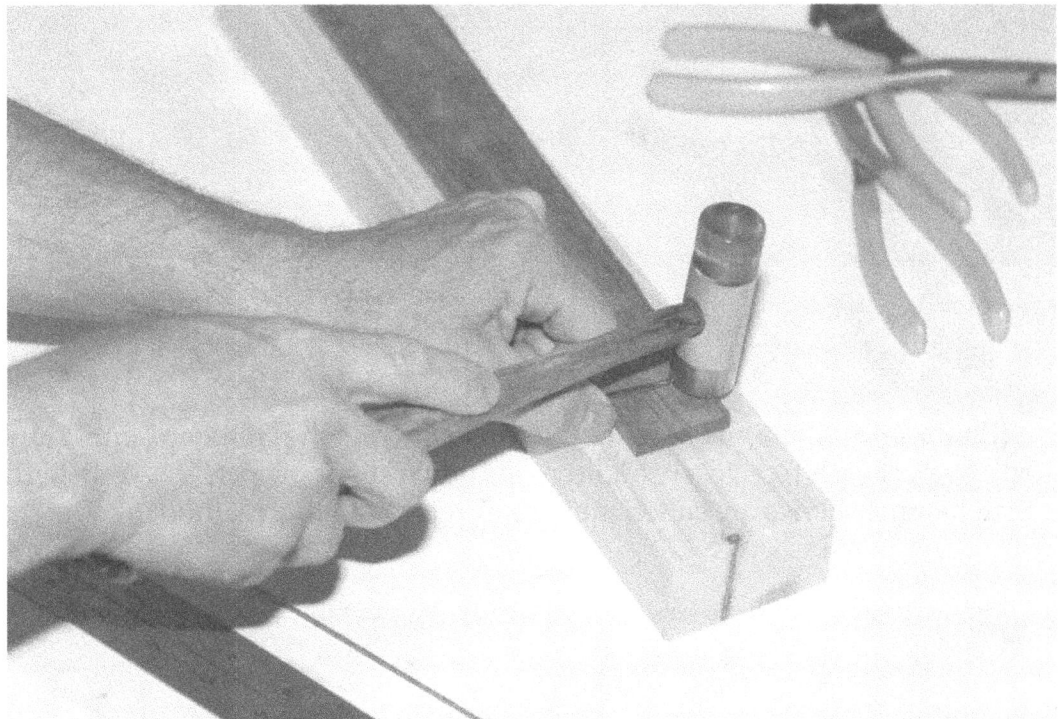

(**Photo 7-14**) Start the fretting process by tapping fret into slot

Some uke builders attach the fretboard to the neck and install frets later in the assembly process. Either method requires some time and patience. I prefer installing the frets before the fingerboard is glued to the neck. This allows you to sand the edge of the fretboard with the frets installed a do much of the shaping of the ends of the frets. The fret ends can be dressed with less obstruction by the body. The ends of the frets must be filed to a 30 to 35 degree angle and this process alone is much easier to do before the fretboard is glued to the neck.

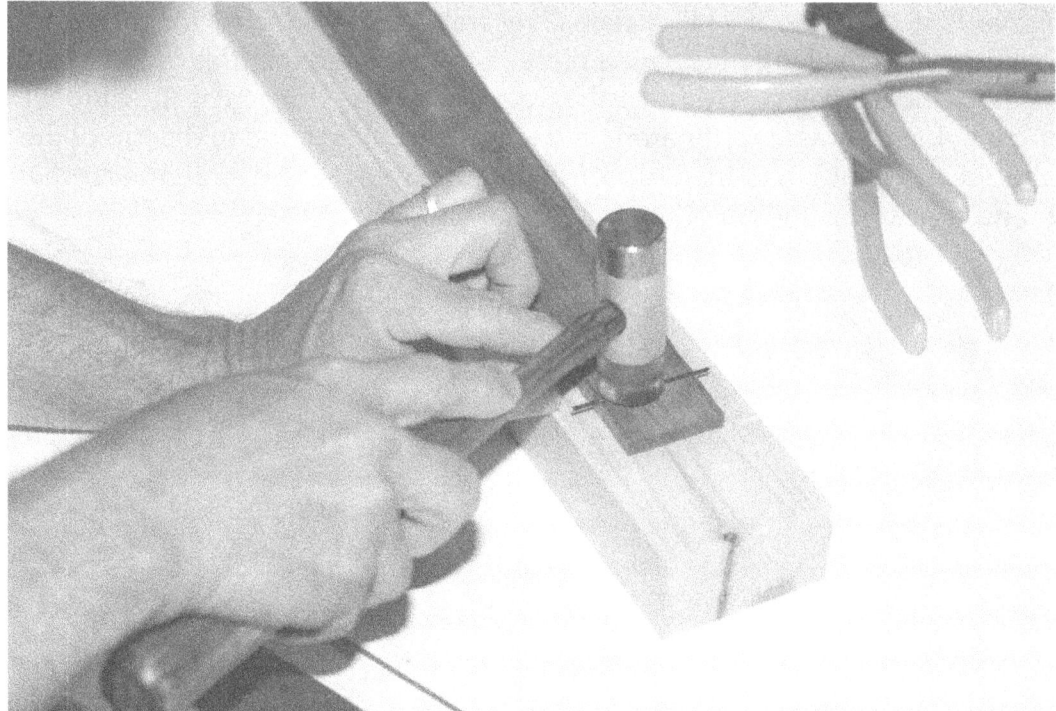

(**Photo 7-15**) Continue hammering the fret across the fretboard until fully seated. Inspect each fret closely and remove any fret not properly seated. Light but firm hammer blows are sufficient to seat frets using this method.

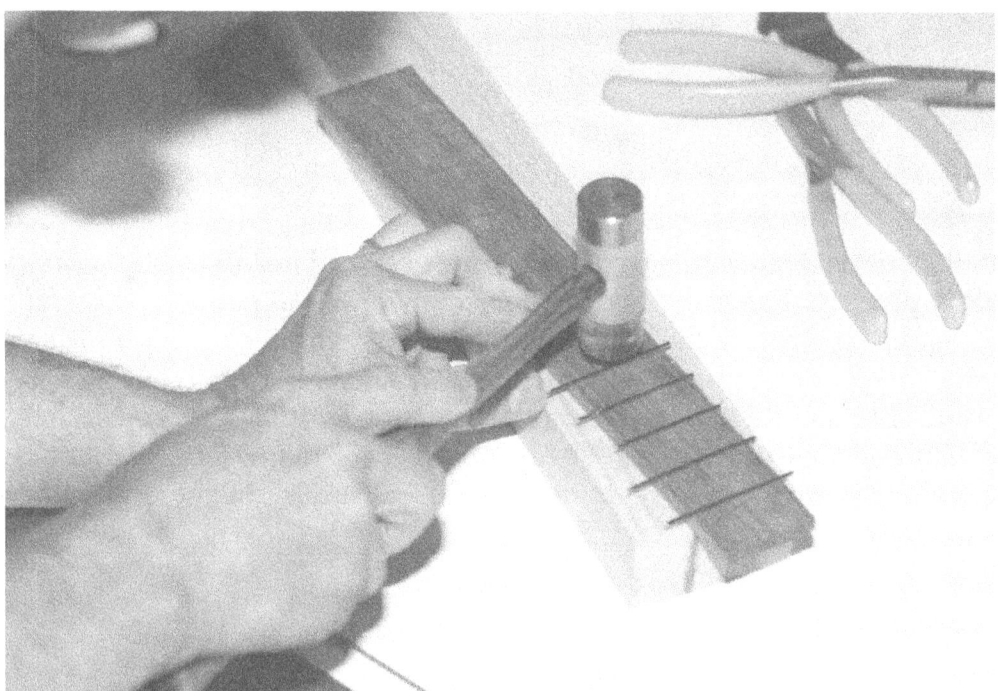

(**Photo 7-16**) Continue to hammer frets into place down the fretboard

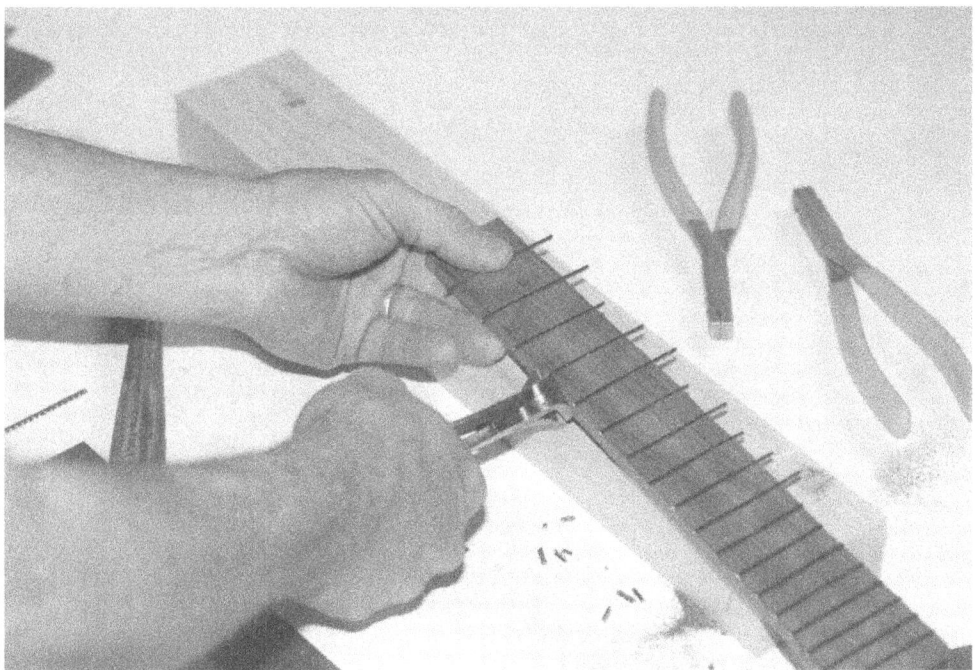

(**Photo 7-17**) Once all of the frets are seated, clip the ends of the fretwire with flush with the edge of the fretboard using flush cutting wire cutters. Before sanding and filing edges of the frets, apply one drop of thin Cyano glue to the end of each fret. It should run under the fret in the fret slots. Use care when applying this glue and do not get it on the fretboard. One way to help protect the fretboard is to apply masking or electrical tape to each side of the frets on the top of the fretboard.

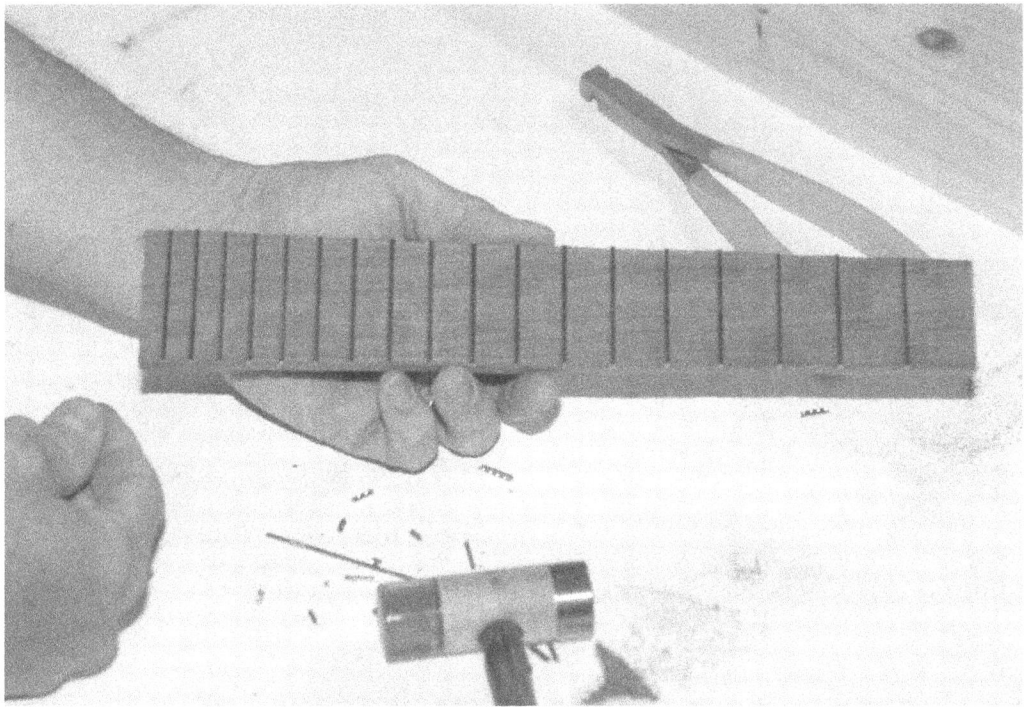

(**Photo 7-17**)   Frets seated and clipped flush with fretboard

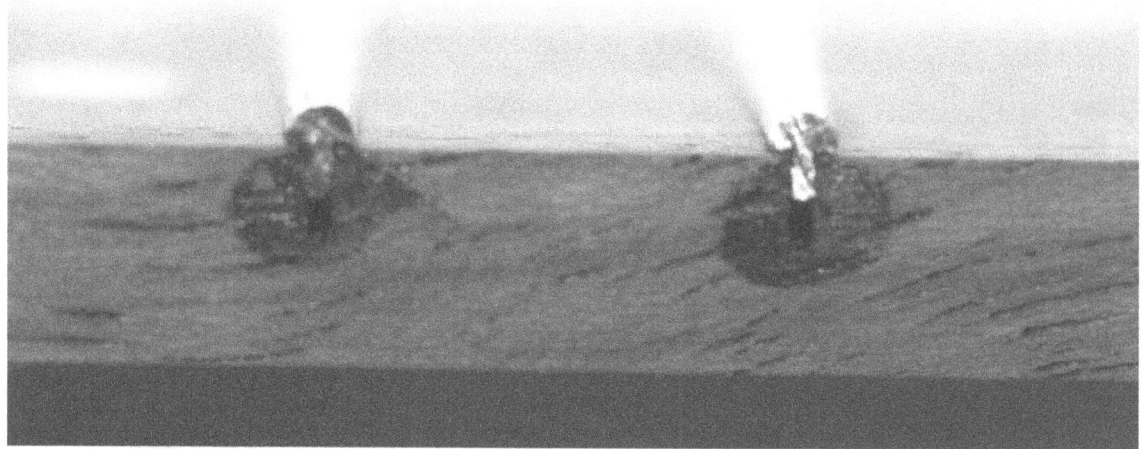

(**Photo 7-18**) Glue applied to ends of fret at edge of fretboard. When dry, the edge of the fretboard can be sanded on edge sander or filled with a large mill file. The frets need to be filed at a 30 degree angle at the end of the frets only and not the fretboard. Each fret will require dressing and rounding over the ends for a smooth feel. The frets might need to be leveled with a sanding block or fine flat mill file. Do not file unless necessary.

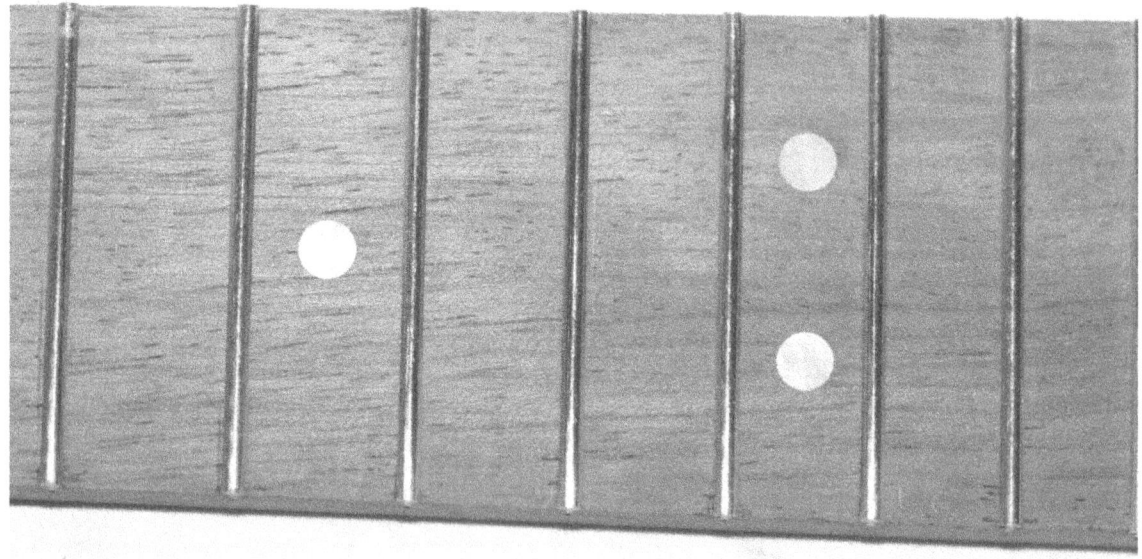

(**Photo 7-19**)   Fretboard is finished for now. Set aside for later.

End of Chapter 7

Chapter 8
Assembly 1

Procedure: Making the Tailblock and Heelblock

The sides are held in alignment by the headblock and the tailblock. These pieces must match the curvature of the body exactly in order to achieve a superior glue joint. The Spanish style construction is concerned only with the tailblock in this section.

Step 1: Making tailblock

Cut a piece of mahogany or maple the height of the sides where they meet at the back seam and the front seam. That is 2- 3/4 inches tall for the heelblock and 3 inches tall for the tailblock. Confirm these dimensions for you instrument. The width is 2-1/2 inches X 3/4 inches + for both pieces.

On the top of the tailblocks draw a line 1/8 inch parallel from one side. Mark the centerline on all for sides. Using the body mold as a template, align the centerline and the edge of the mold at the 1/8 inch mark. Draw that arc on you block on both ends. (See photo 8-2) That will be a perfect pattern of the tailblock.

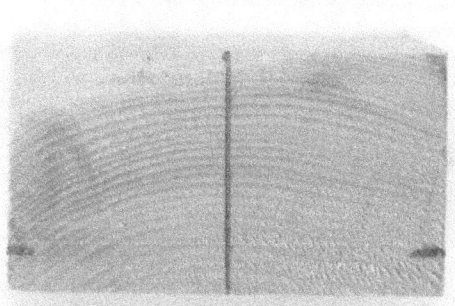

(**Photo 8-1**)   Find the centerline and the 1/8 inch marks

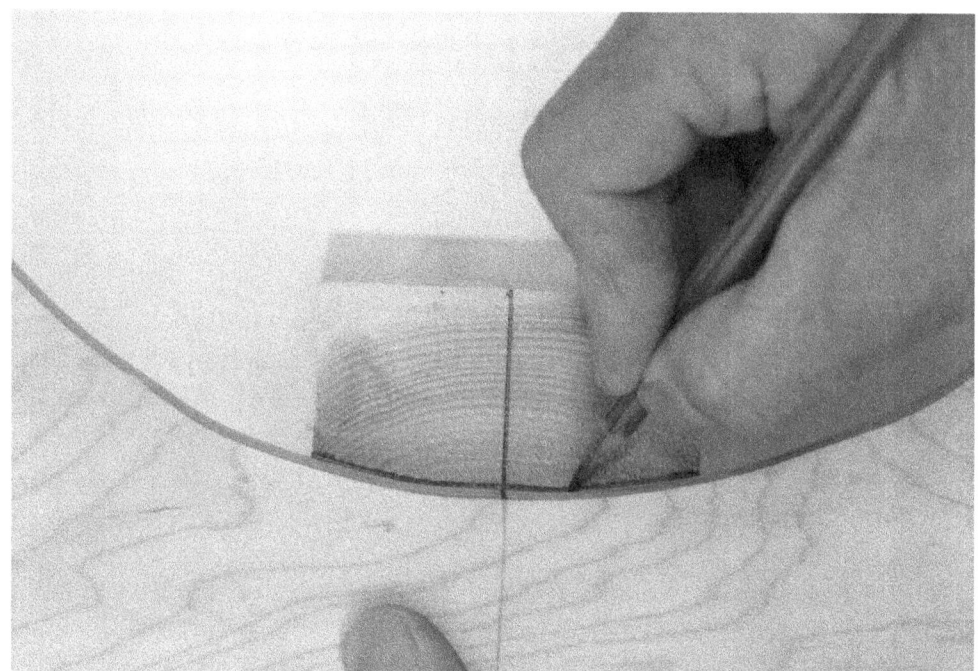

(**Photo 8-2**)   Marking the curvature of the mold at the centerline at tailpiece

The tailblock is to be sanded on the sander or sawn and sanded smooth. First attach a "handle" to the back of the tailpiece using a small block with double sided tape. This is to keep you hand away from the sander.

(**Photo 8-3**) Handle attached to the tailblock and the radius is sanded to match the mold. (see **Photo 8-2**) This block should match the mold exactly and will be glued to the side where they meet.

Step 2: Heelblock & Tailblock

There is no separate heelblock used with Spanish style construction. The Box style heelblock is square to accept the neck with it's square end. There is a flat area on the soundbox that is about 3inches wide that need to be sanded flat. The heelblock is only slightly rounded on the two edges that will come into contact with the sides. Notice the flat areas on outline of body template.

Procedure: Gluing sides to tailblock

Step 1: Insert the sides in the body mold for the box style or into the slots in the Spanish style neck. Allow them to overlap and mark.

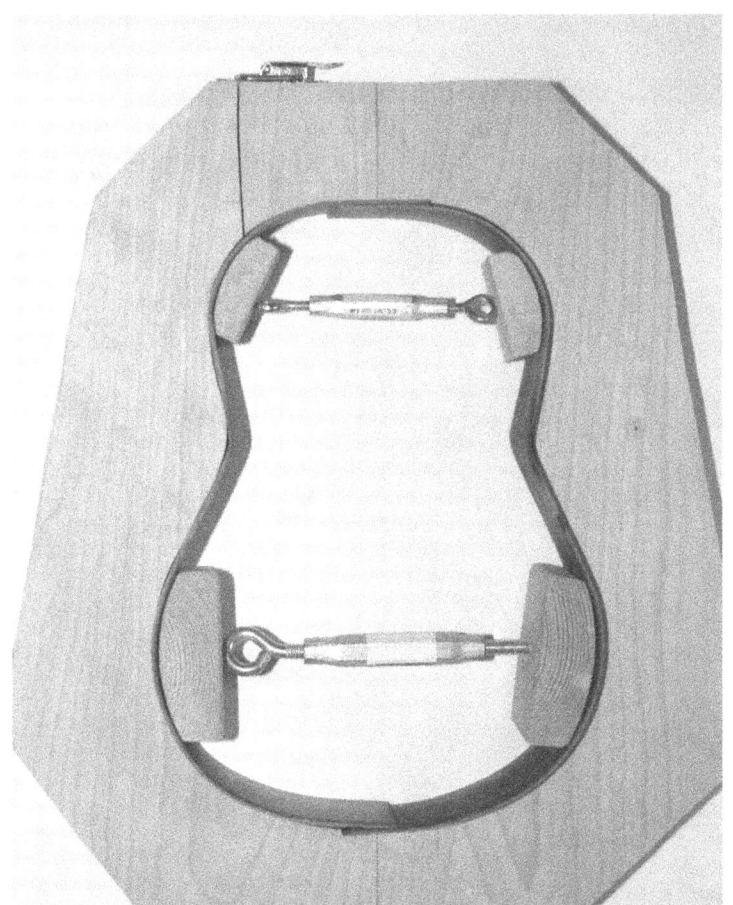

(**Photo 8-4**) The sides are inserted into the body mold. Mark sides where they overlap and scribe a line square to the top side of the sides. The bottom of the sides have a taper so the marks not allow a square mark. Cut the sides close and sand up. While sanding, check the fit often.

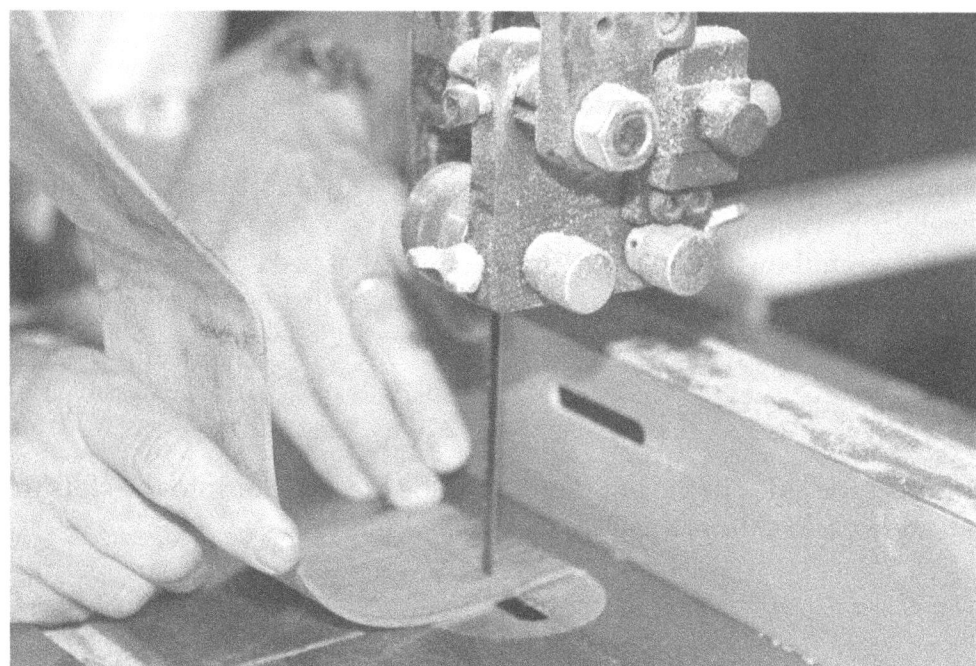

(**Photo 8-5**) The sides being cut to length on bandsaw. The next step is to sand to the line. Cut the sides a little long and test fit to obtain a tight joint where the two halves of the side meet.

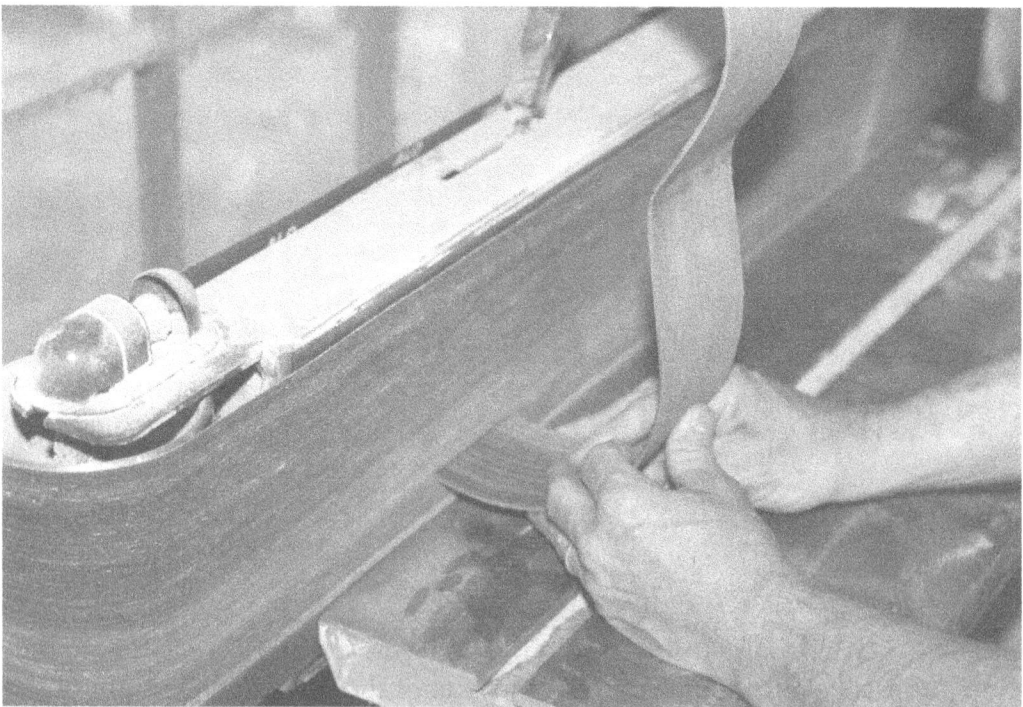

(**Photo 8-6**) Sanding side to fit at centerline of the mold

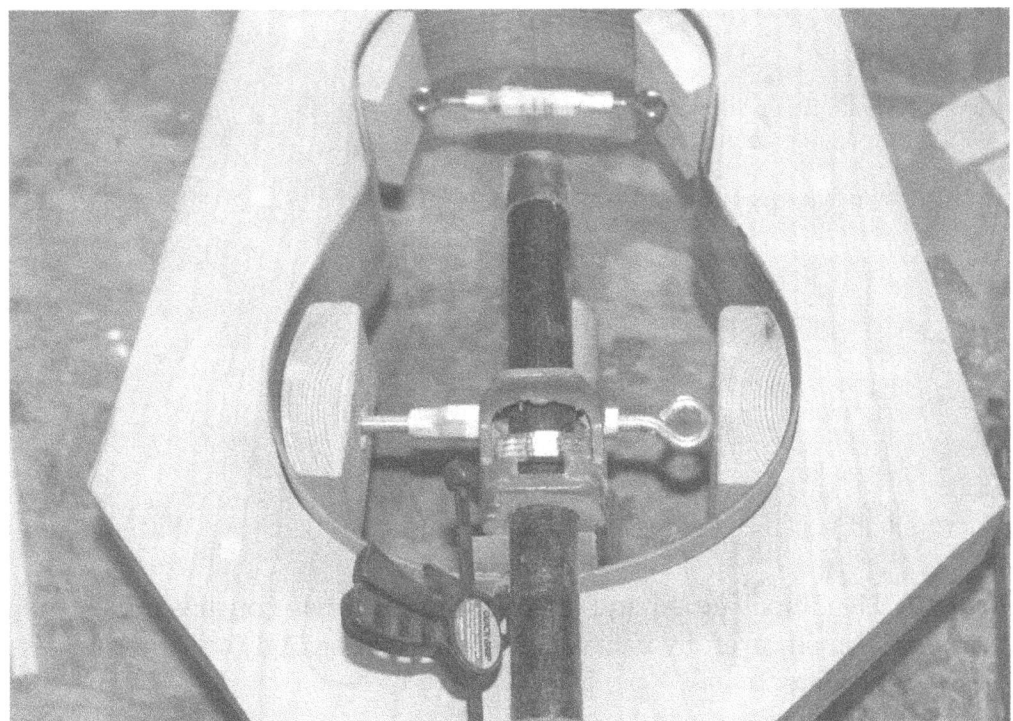

(**Photo 8-7**) Tailblock clamped to sides in mold. Notice that a pipe clamp is used for this step. A pipe clamp allows you to exert much more pressure during this important step.

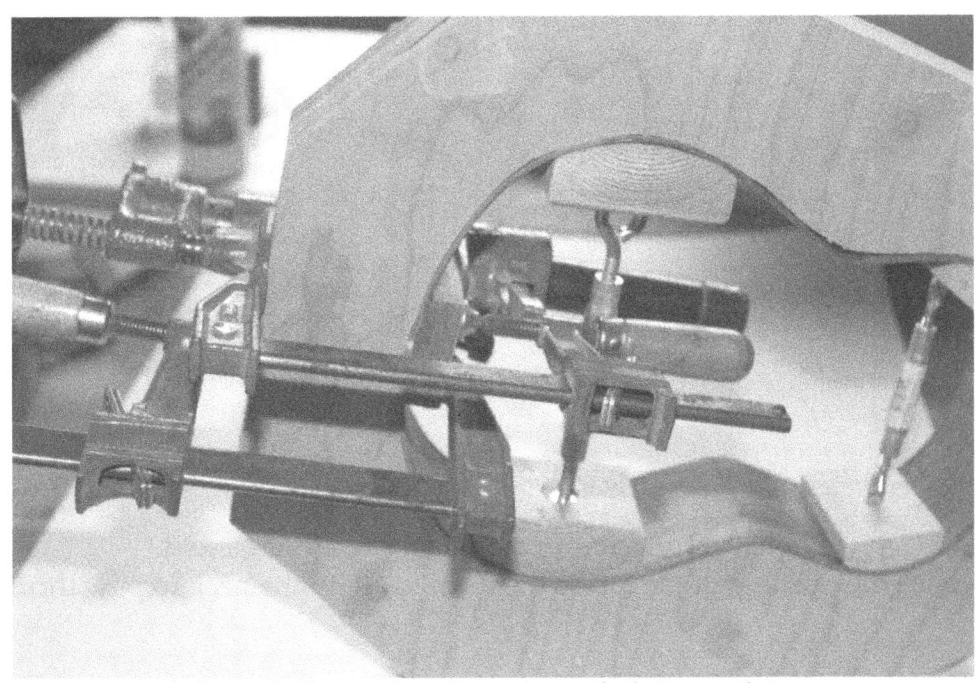

(**Photo 8-8**)   Another view of gluing tailpiece

(**Photo 8-10**) Headblock glued and clamped for box style construction. This area needs to be clamped carefully because it is flat for about 1-1/4 inches on each side of the centerline.

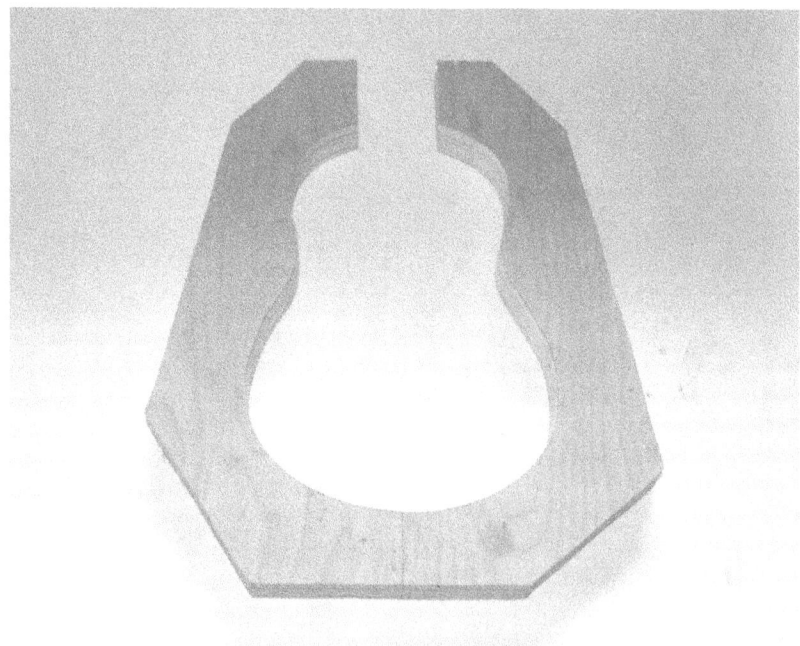

(**Photo 8-11**) A view of a Spanish style body mold. Notice the opening of the top of the form to allow the neck to pass thru.

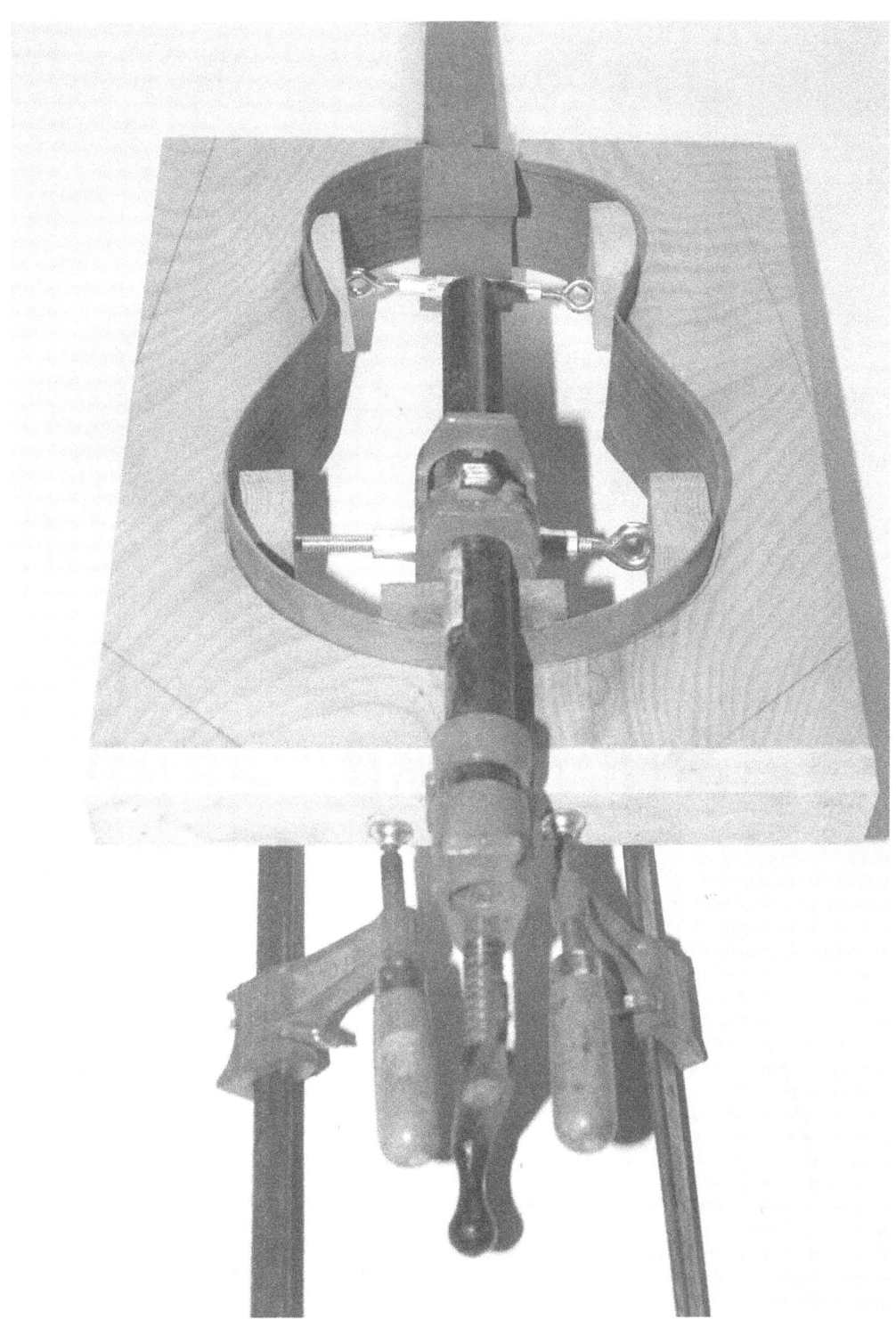

(Photo 8-12) The tailblock glued to sides in a Spanish style mold. The mold is basically the same as box style but it has a space for the integral neck to pass thru.

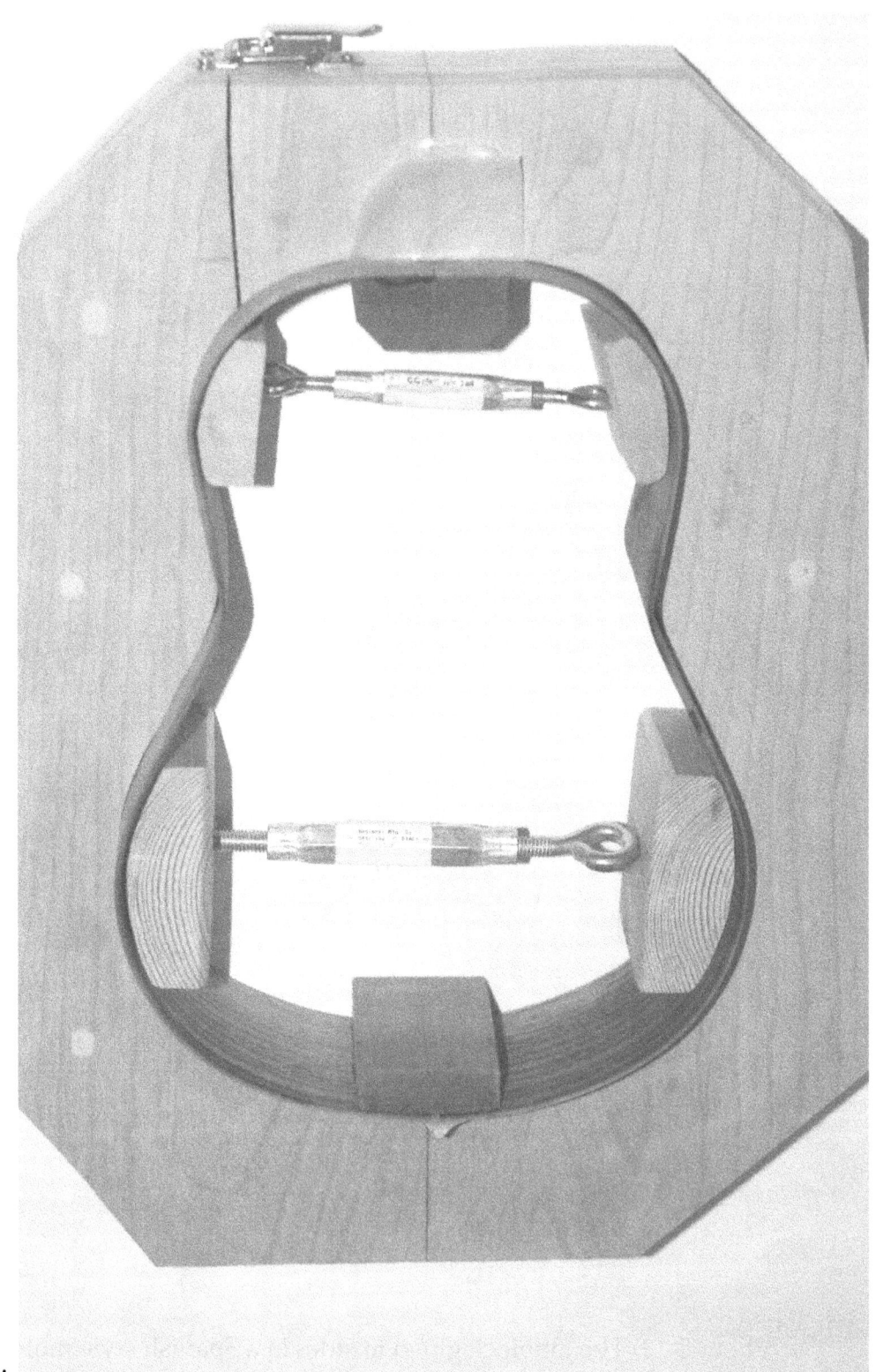

(**Photo 8-13**) Headblock and tailblock glued and secured in mold. Don't forget the wax paper. The sides remain in the mold for the next several steps.

Step 2: Sanding the top and bottom edges flat to prepare for installing kerfing

Now that the sides are glued to the heelblock and tailblock, the top and bottom edges must be sanded to accept the kerfing for the soundboard and the back. The top will be sanded flat on the sanding board. (See *Jigs*) Remember that the soundboard was built flat. The sides will be sanded in the mold and remain there for the installation of the kerfing.

The back has two planes to sand. The first is from the high point on the side which is two inches in front of the waist line to the front of the instrument. This point is marked on the sides from our layout and bending the sides. The other sanding plane is from the high point of the sides to the back of the instrument. When sanding the back attention should be given to the two sanding planes. For now, we will sand the edges flat to prepare to install the kerfing.

(**Photo 8-14**) Sanding the top edges with the sides in the mold and an extra clamp at the heelblock and tailblock. Sand until sides and heelblock and tailblock are one plane. As an aid, draw white pencil marks around the sides, heelblock and tailblock. When the pencil marks are gone, the bottom is sanded flat.

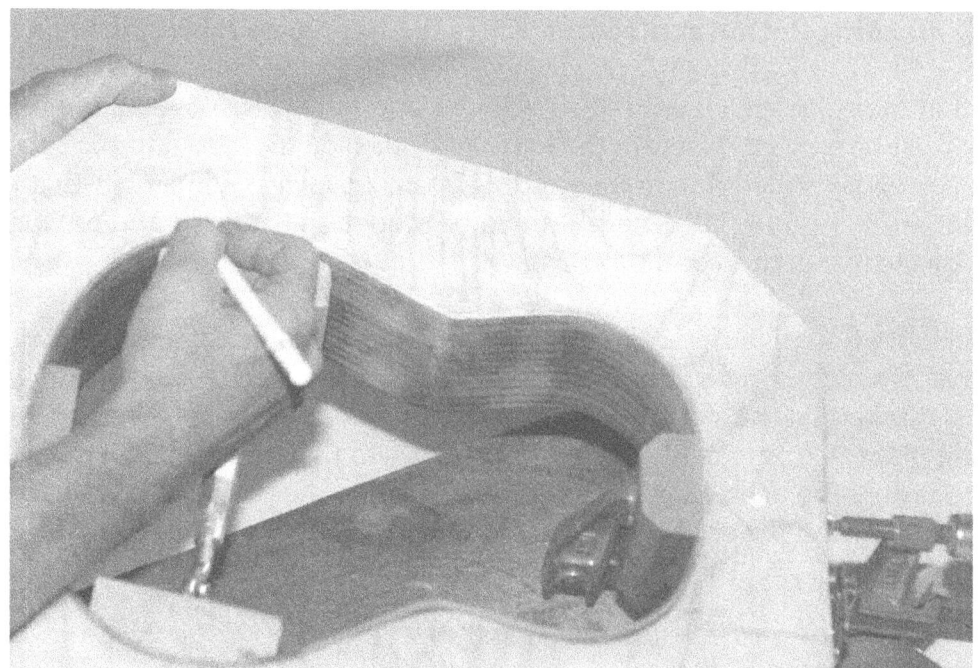

(**Photo 8-15**) Marking edges and tailblock and heelblock with white pencil. When the pencil marks are gone the top is flat.

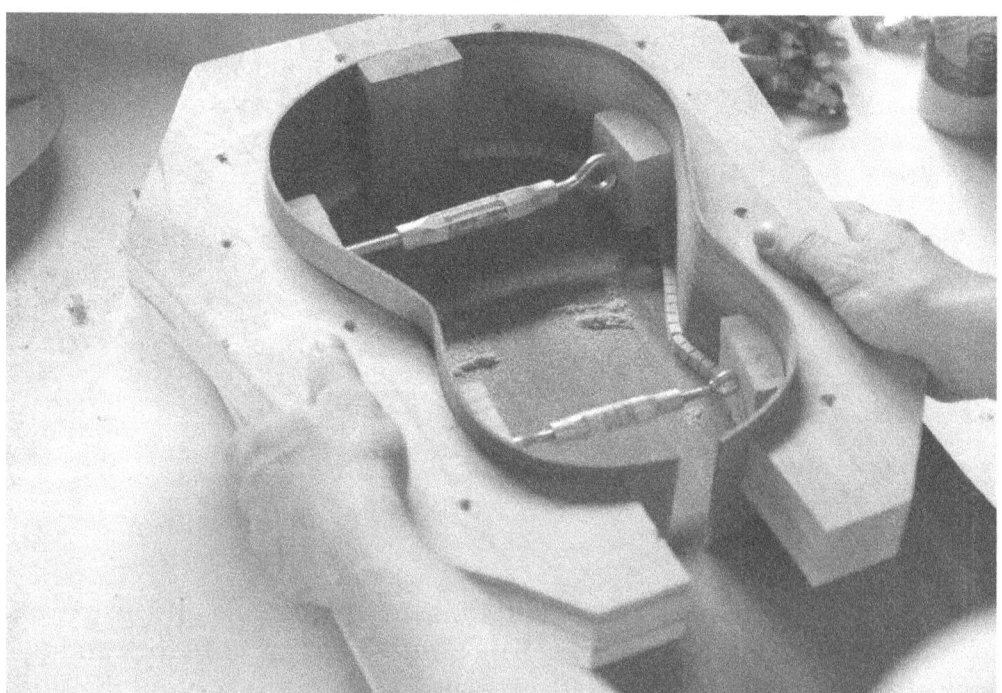

(**Photo 8-16**) Sanding the edges of side of a Spanish style body. The ends of the sides will be inserted into the grooves of the Spanish style neck later. (see **Photo 8-12**)

Step 3: Gluing and sanding kerfing

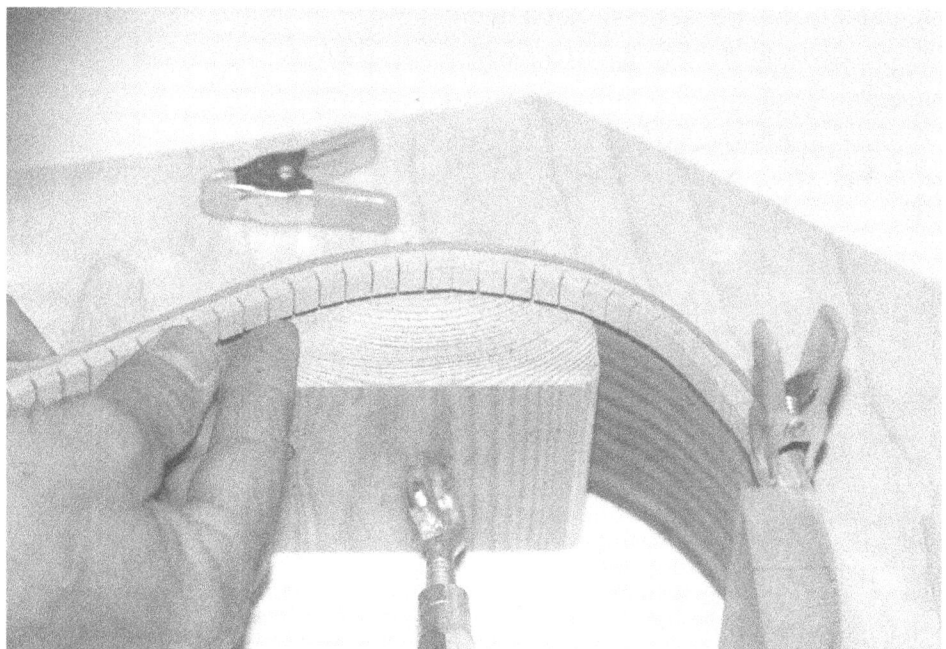

(Photo 8-17)   Check the fit of the kerfing along top of side

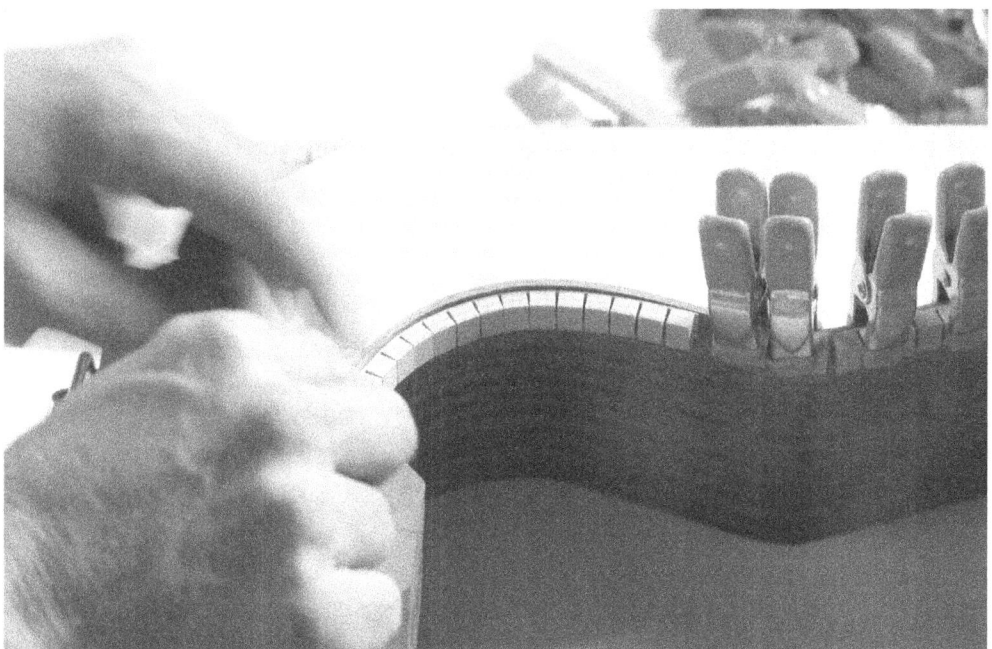

(Photo 8-18) Start gluing kerfing along the top edge of the side. The kerfing should protrude about 1/32+ inch beyond the top of the side. This will allow for room to sand the kerfing exactly level with the sides and tailblock and heelblock.

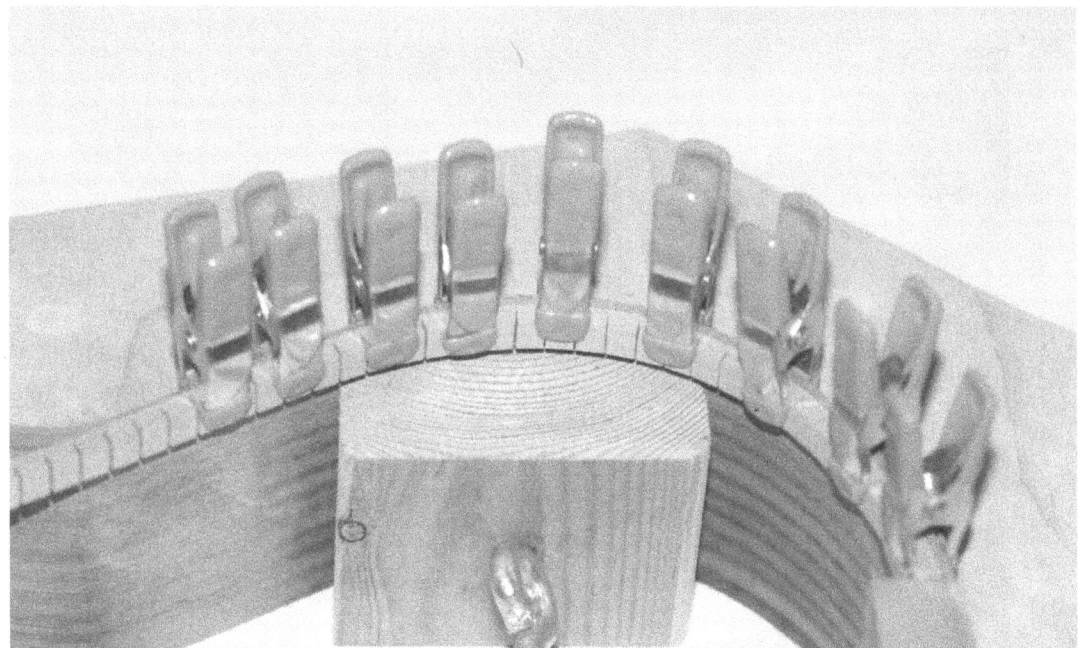

(Photo 8-19) Continue gluing the kerfing with Titebond and clamping every 1/4 inch completely around the top. The kerfing does not need to be one continuous piece. Just make the joints tight. You can clamp the kerfing dry to help form the curves. The small clamps must be strong enough to hold the kerfing tight to the sides. Using clothes pins for clamps is not recommended. Allow ample time for the glue to dry.

Kerfing is often referred to as *tentalones* or *kerfed lining*. Kerfing is available in several sizes. The small square kerfing is best suited for ukuleles and is slightly easier to clamp than triangular shape.

Some uke builders do not use kerfing on the bottom where the back meets the sides. Instead, *lining* is used. Lining is simply a narrow strip of the same material as the sides formed the same as the sides. Often times lining is cut from the steam-bent sides. The lining strips can be bent on the side bending jig in a separate step. Wood binding can also be bent on the side bending jig . Bending the lining and binding on the side bending jig will assure a perfect contour and a good fit during installation.

My preference is 1/4 x 5/16 inch spruce kerfing available from suppliers in 30 to 36 inch lengths. You can make your own kerfing if you make a jig for cutting the kerfing. The slots should be evenly spaced with very narrow saw kerfs slightly less than 1/16 inch.

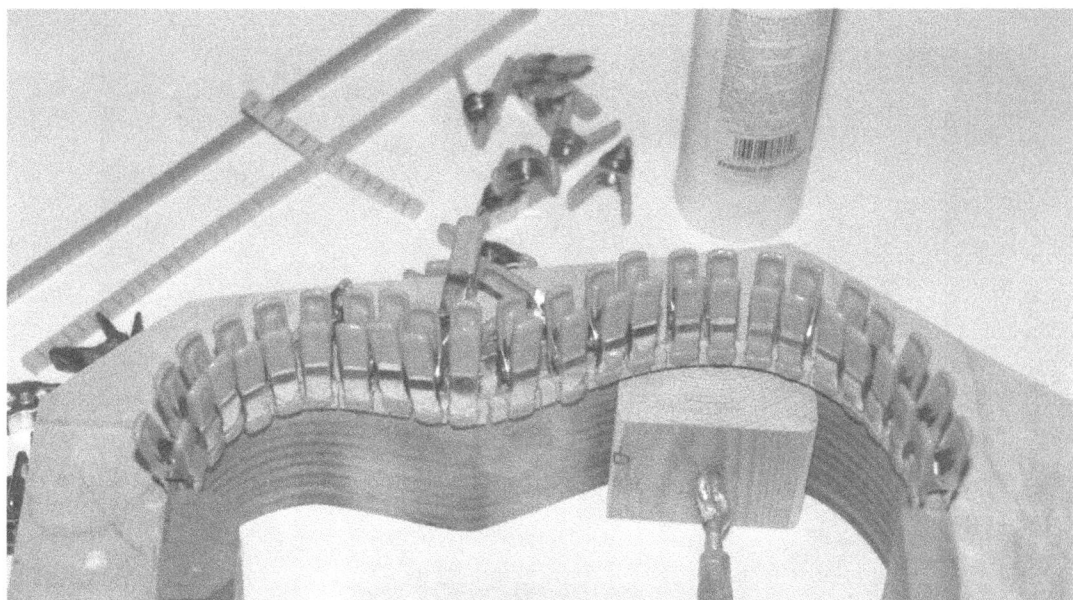

(**Photo 8-20**) One side of the kerfing glued and clamped from block to block. Repeat the process for the other side of the top. Allow to dry several hours. Remove all clamps and prepare to sand on sanding board. Sand as before by marking the sides and blocks with pencil and sand until marks are gone. Wait to sand until after both sides are glued and dry.

(**Photo 8-21**) A close-up view of the sanded side and kerfing. Sawdust almost hides the cuts in the kerfing. This side is ready to be cleaned, fitted and attach the soundboard.

The back sides are glued and sanded the same way. Remember that the back has two different planes to sand level. You may need to cut the thin back or the kerfing to allow for the two different level surfaces.

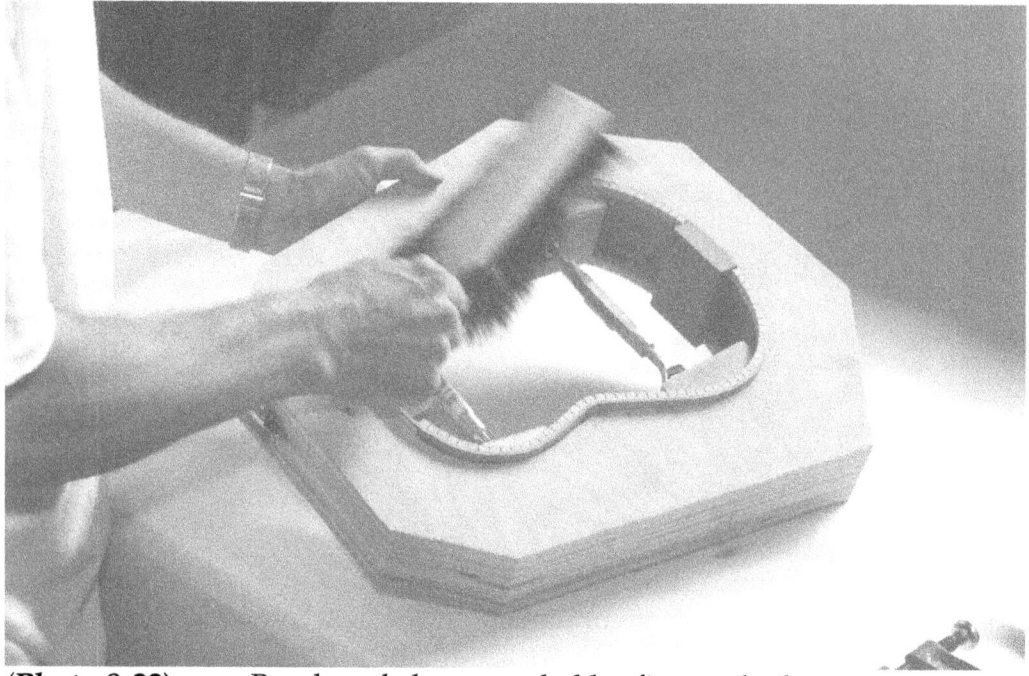

(**Photo 8-22**)　　Brush and clean sanded kerfing and edges

Step 4: Fitting and attaching soundboard

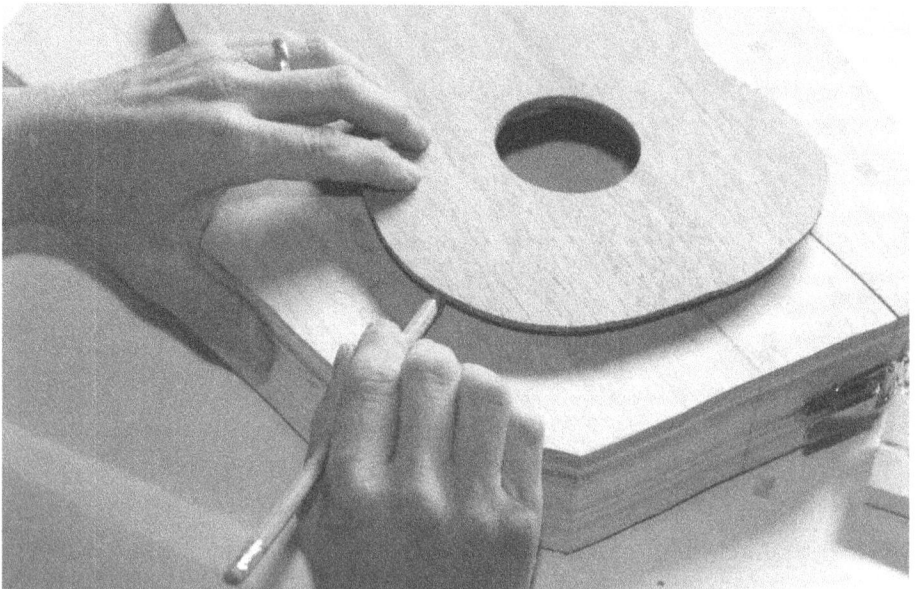

(**Photo 8-23**) Mark kerfing where the soundboard braces touch. The braces will be trimmed and tapered to fit into kerfing.

(**Photo 8-24**) A notch in the kerfing to accept a soundboard brace. A small piece of kerfing will be replaced over the brace.

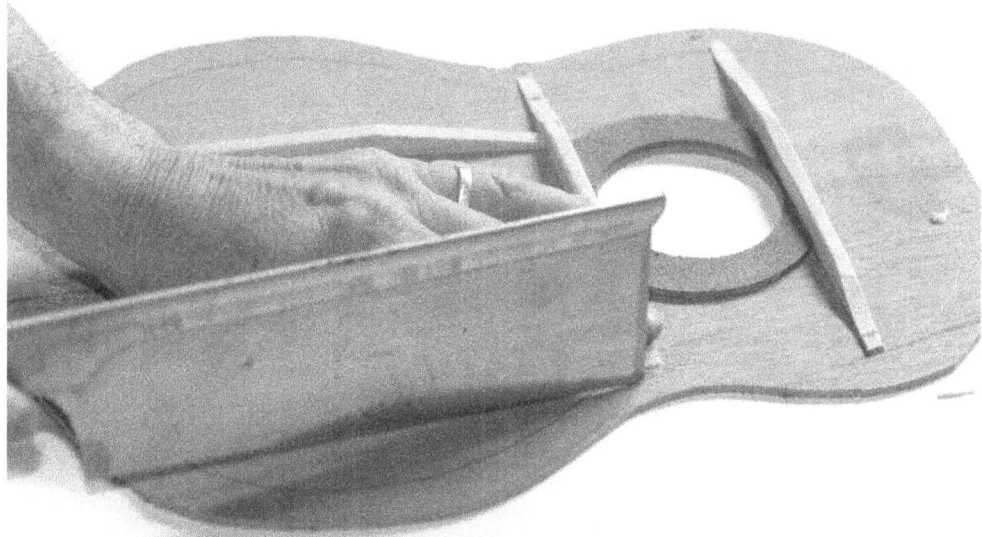

(**Photo 8-25**) Soundboard braces being cut to match outline of pattern. The braces should be cut a little long to allow extra wood to taper brace to meet soundboard. Mark the soundboard outline and cut soundboard bracing at lines. The braces will fit into small notches cut in the kerfing with Dremel tool.

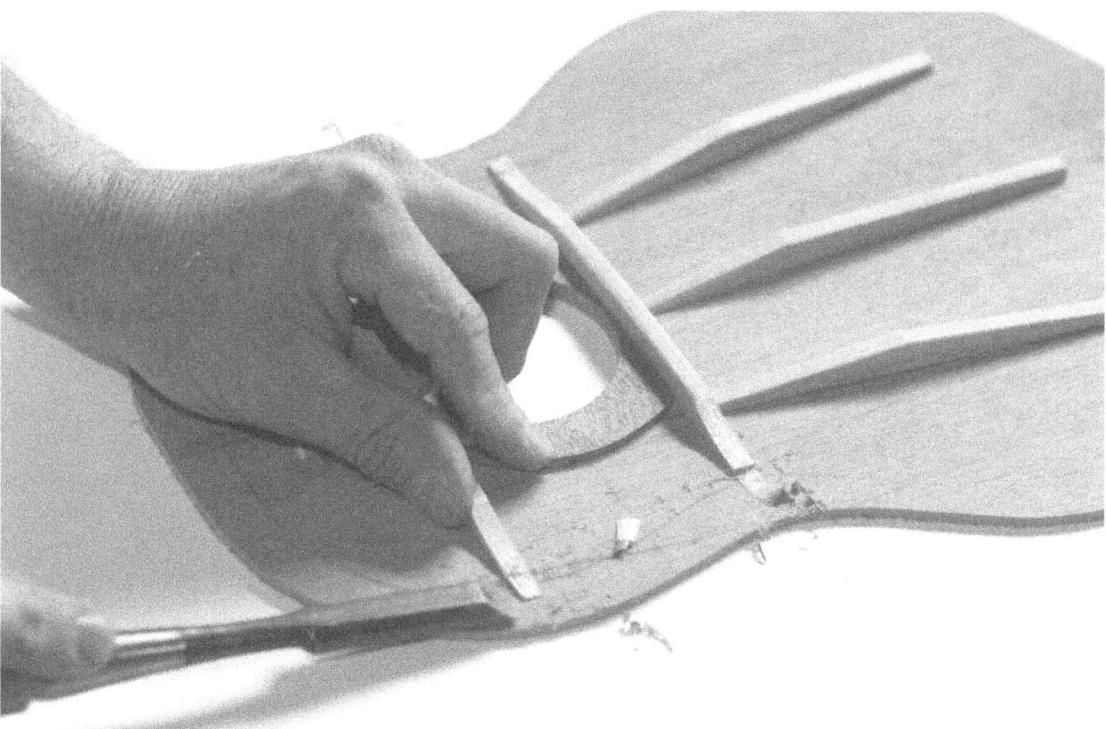

(**Photo 8-26**)   Braces being shortened to outline of pattern. Use care during this step and cut with the grain of the soundboard when using the chisel.

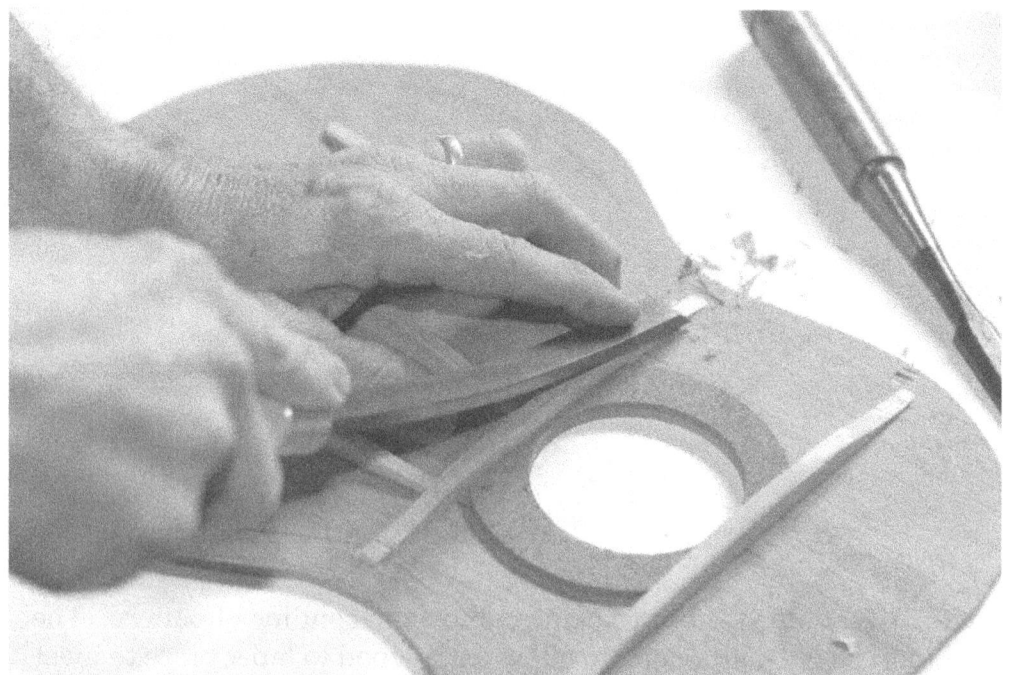

(**Photo 8-27**) Trimmed braces being tapered to the surface of soundboard. leave about 1/16 inch thickness at the ends of the braces. They will later be tucked in a pocket in the kerfing in preparation of gluing the top to sides.

Step 5: Gluing soundboard to sides

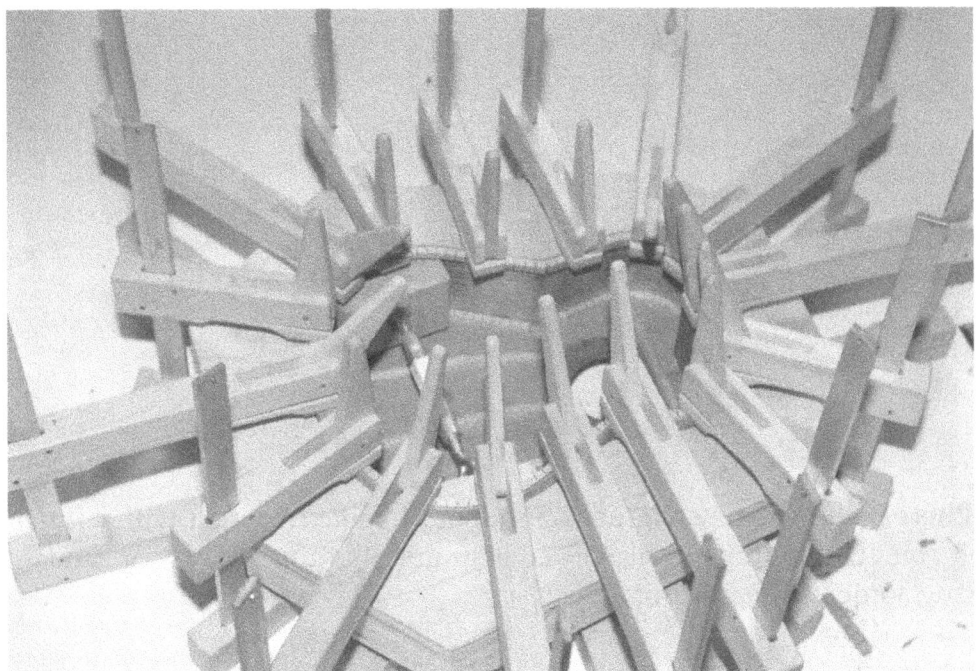

(**Photo 8-28**) A major milestone! The front is glued and clamped to the sides. Clamps must be evenly spaced with moderate pressure. Check for a flush fit during a dry fit. If you are satisfied glue and clamp the top. Allow to dry several hours.

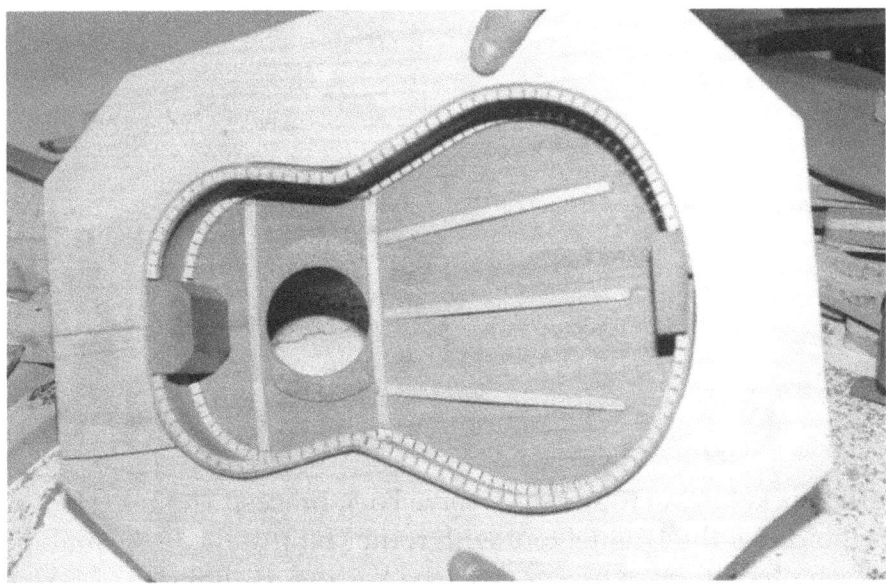

(**Photo 8-29**) The braced soundboard glued to the sides. As always, the centerlines should all line up. This is the Box style body. It will remain in the mold until the top is glued to the body.

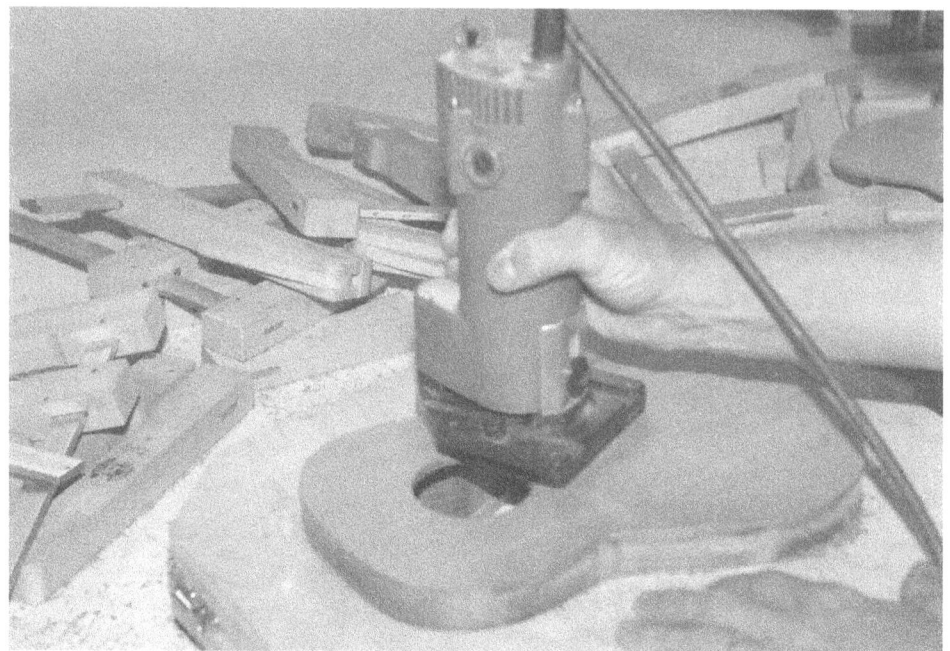

(**Photo 8-30**) The newly glued soundboard being trimmed with a flush cutting bit. Use caution with short edge grain. It is good to saw or sand overhang some before routing.

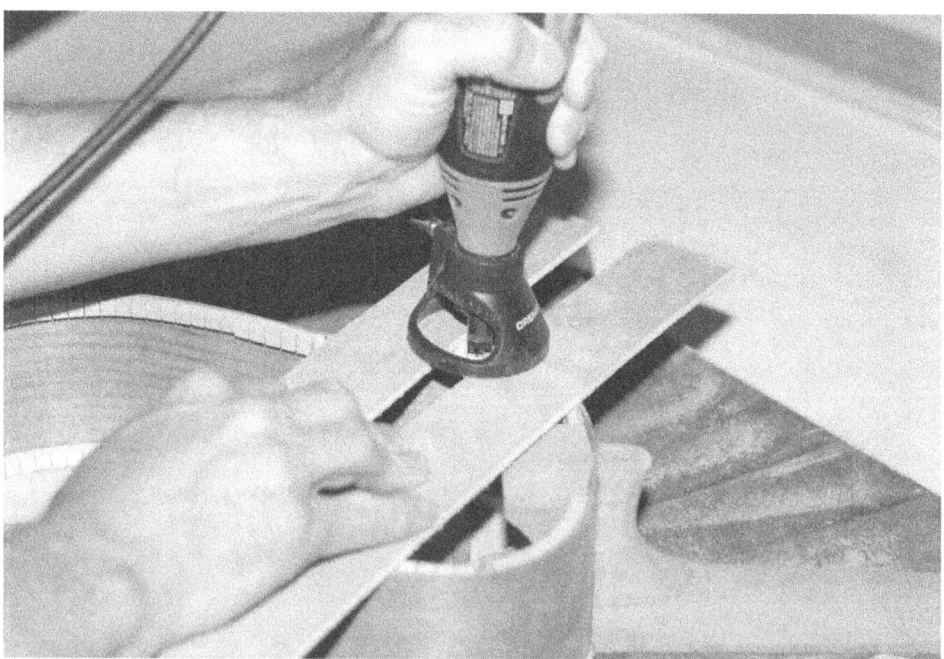

(**Photo 8-31**) Pocket being routed to receive back braces. The two slats act as a temporary guide for the Dremel tool with router bit installed. A small pocket is routed at each place that the braces meet the kerfing on the back. Make this fit as tight as possible. There is no room to add a small piece of kerfing like on the soundboard now that the back will be glued in place.

UKULELE Design & Construction

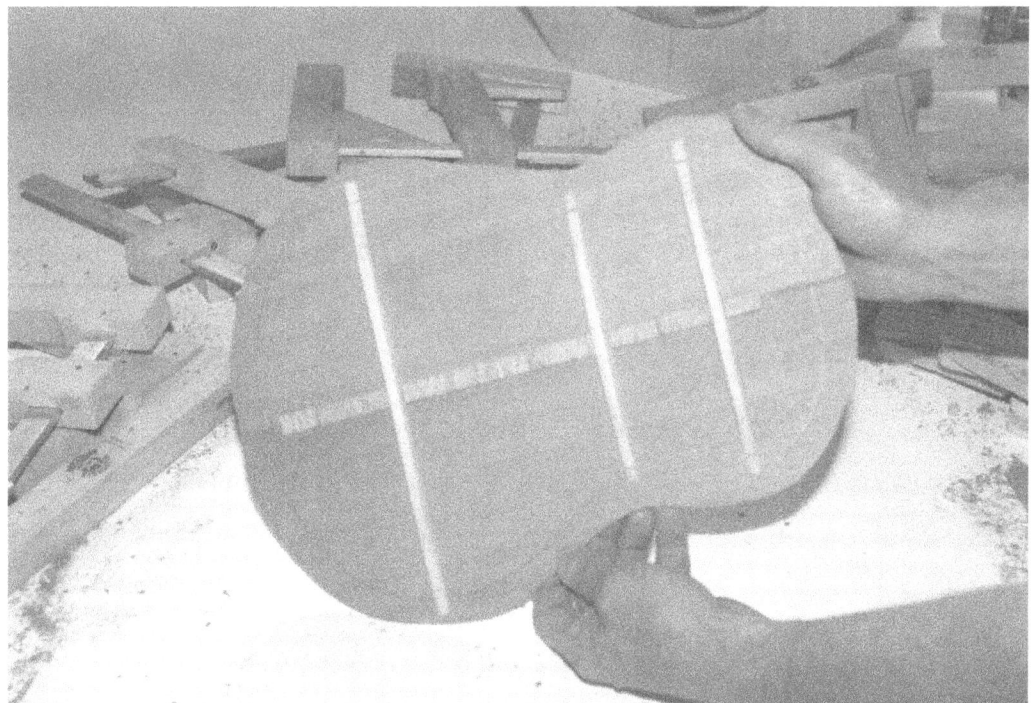

(**Photo 8-32**) The back has back seam graft in place and is ready to be fitted for installation. Repeat the process used in preparing and gluing the soundboard.

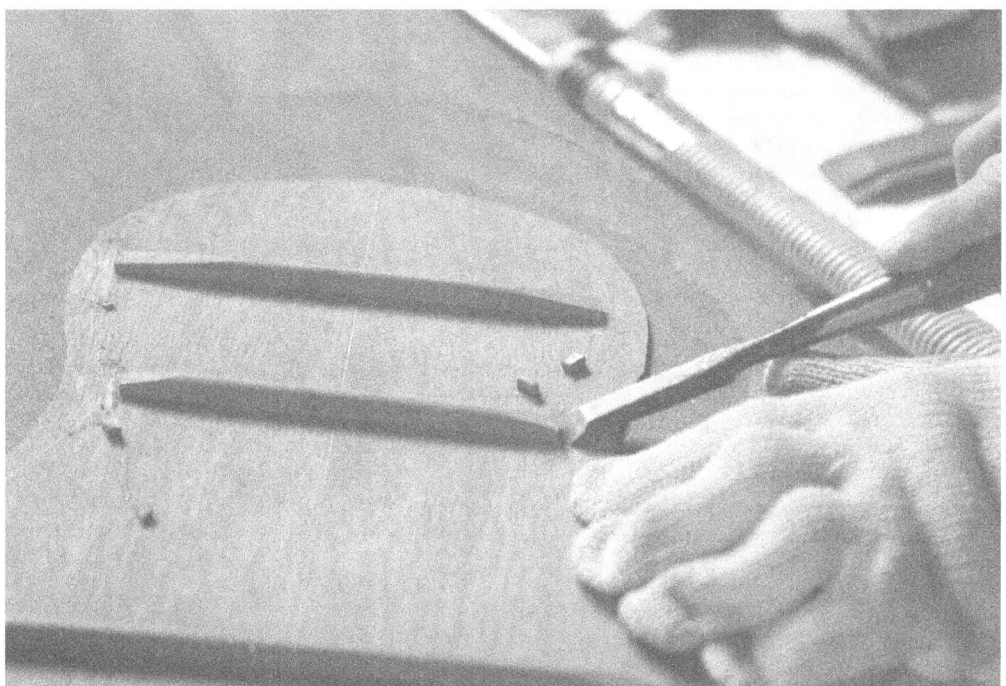

(**Photo 8-33**) Removing excess back brace length while wearing a Kevlar glove for protection from the chisel. As with the soundboard, use caution while removing the excess brace material from the back. It is somewhat safer to chisel with the grain of the back. Use only a very sharp chisel.

91

(**Photo 8-34**) The back is glued and clamped. Allow several hours to dry. Align the clamps directly over the sides and do not let the clamps extend past the sides too far.

(**Photo 8-35**) <u>Careful when sawing off excess back</u>. The taper and arch that is built into back will not allow the body to lay flat on the saw table. It will not be a 90 degree cut. Use caution so as not to cut into the sides. When the excess is sawed away, it is best to flush up the edge of the back with wood rasps and sanding.

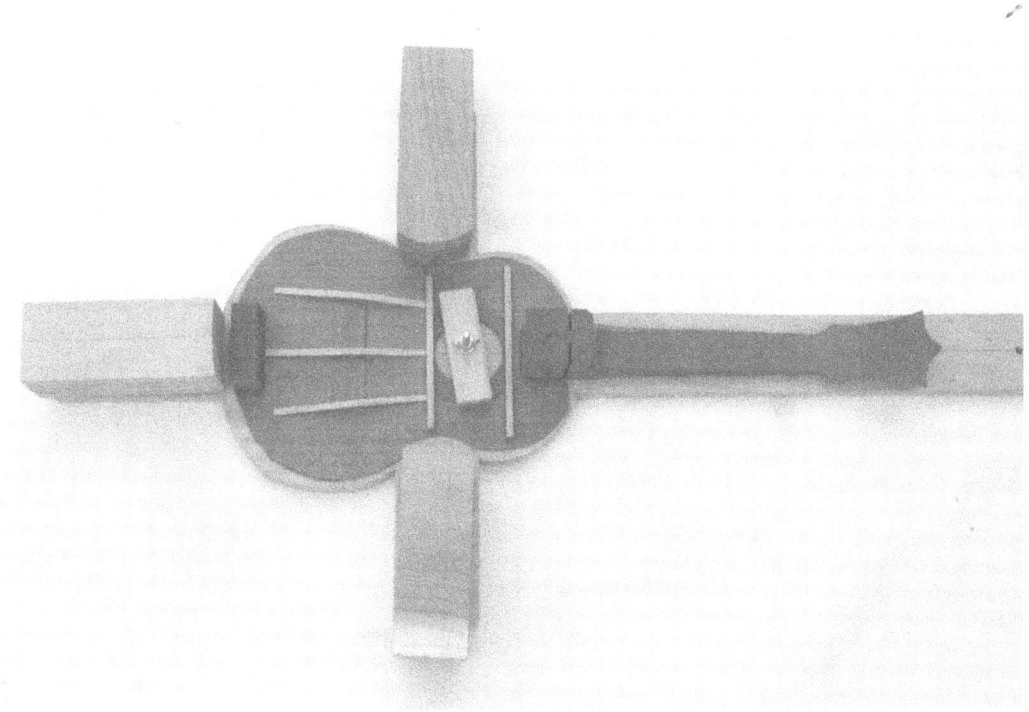

(**Photo 8-36**)   Spanish Style neck alignment jig ready for sides

(**Photo 8-37**) Gluing neck to sides with the help of the *Neck Alignment* jig

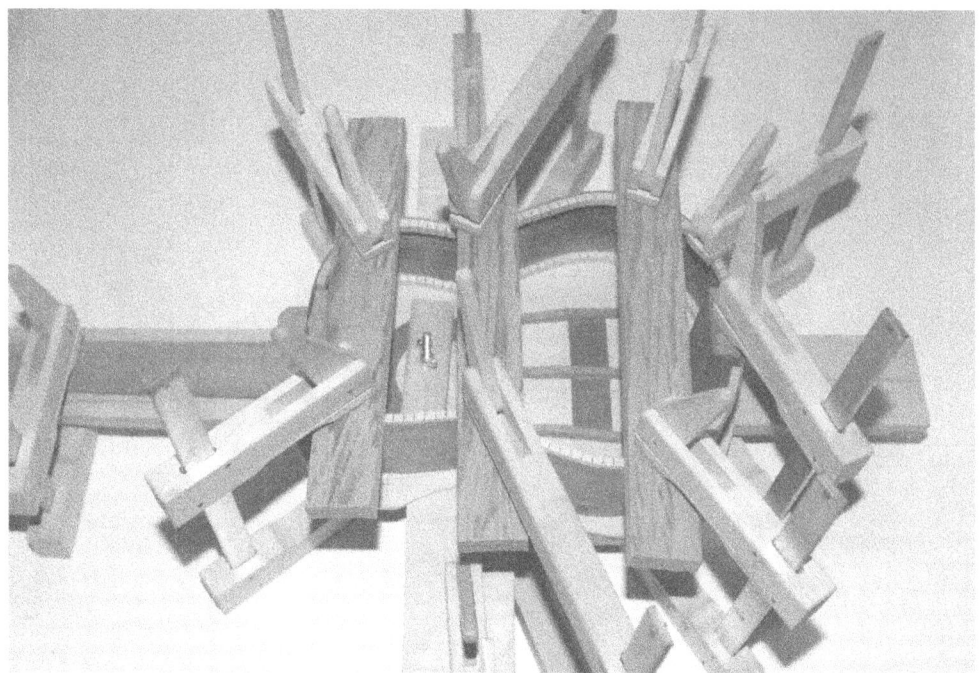
(**Photo 8-38**)   Gluing sides to soundboard with Spanish style neck

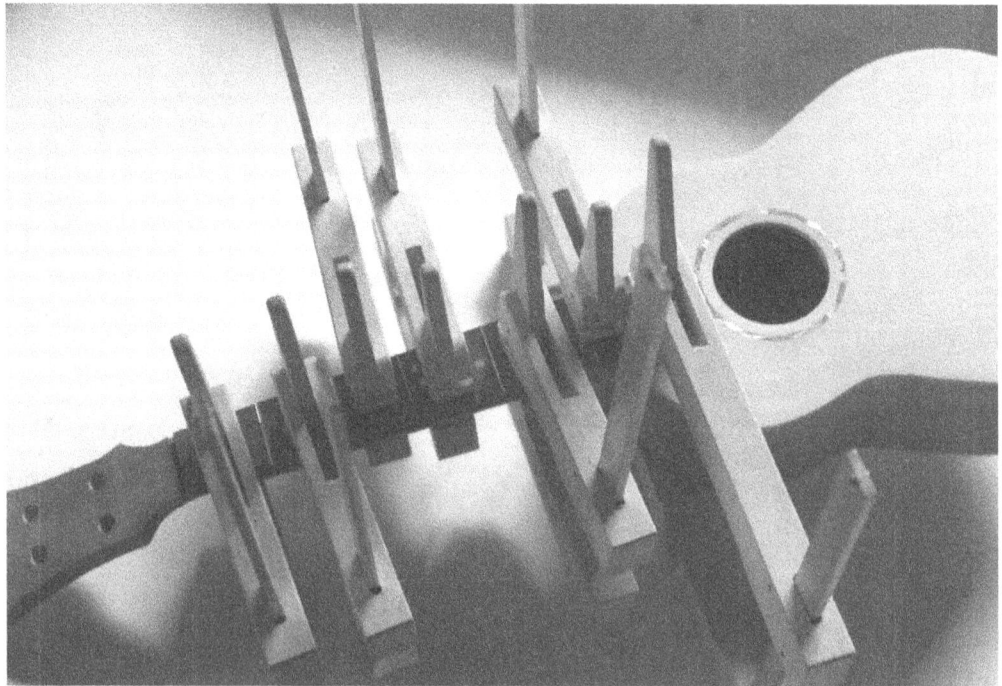
(**Photo 8-39**) Fretboard glued and clamped to Spanish style neck

End of Chapter 8

Chapter 9
End Graft

The end graft is usually an inlay of wood or ivoroid that is at the point where the two halves of the sides meet at the tailblock. It is totally optional but dose add an element and a chance to use dissimilar material. Sometime the end graft serves the purpose of covering up a not so perfect seam of the sides.

Procedure: Making and installing an end graft

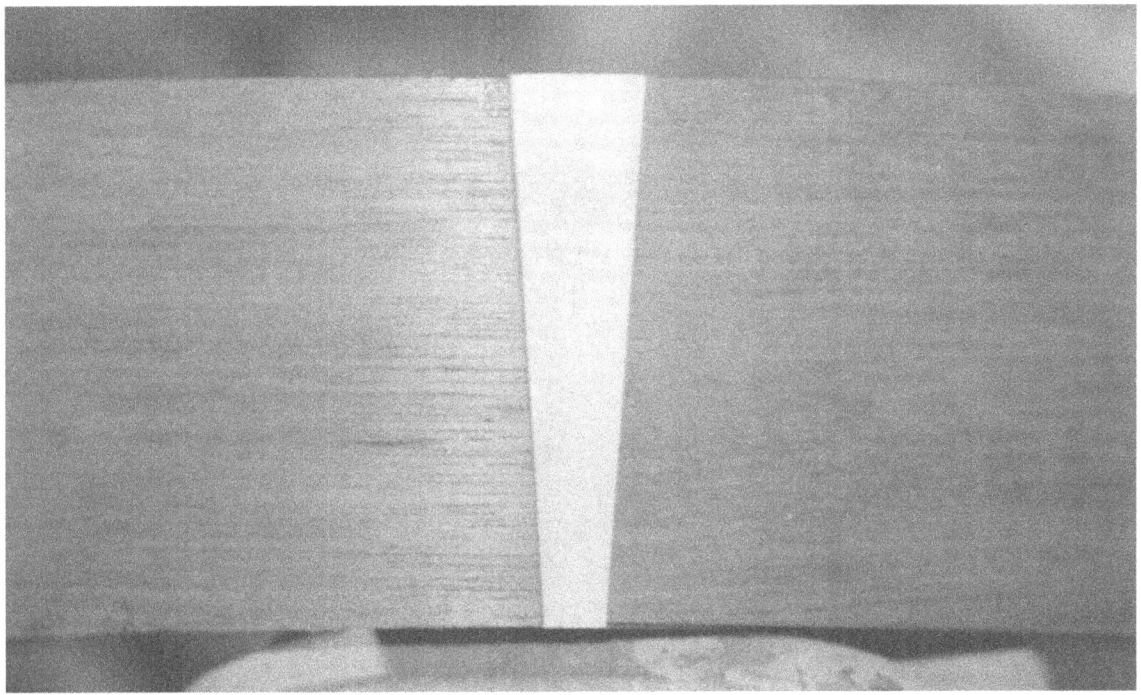

(**Photo 9-1**) An example of an end graft. The inlay material used here is scrap Sitka spruce from the soundboard. The end graft is often not tapered as pictured.

Step 1: Layout and scribe the shape of the inlay

This end graft is 3/4 inch at the top and 3/8 inch at the bottom. The end of the ukulele is 3 inches. Working from the centerline, lay out the taper and mark the points with an awl. Next, using a marking knife, mark the two tapered lines. Use the groove made by the marking knife to start your cut. A Japanese dovetail saw is the very best because it cuts on the pull stroke and it gives you so much control.

(**Photo 9-2**) Cutting along the marks with dovetail saw. Notice the not so perfect seams that will disappear with the addition of the end graft.

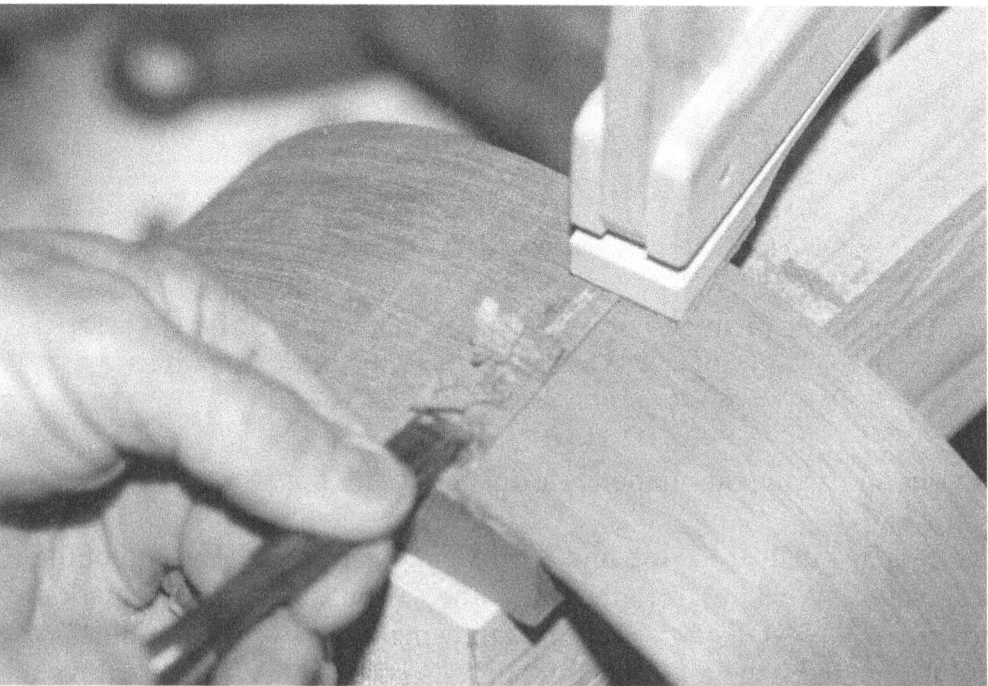

(**Photo 9-3**) The outer boundaries have been cut and now is the time to chisel. Remove only the wood from the sides. Do not cut into the tailblock.

(**Photo 9-4**) Switch to narrow chisel for the top section. Try to keep the out lines straight and square because we have an insert to mate to the cut.

(**Photo 9-5**) The carving is finished and we have a good channel with sharp, straight sides that will make a nice joint.

(Photo 9-6) A tapered spruce inlay is gently tapped into place.

The more pressure on the spruce the tighter the joint. It is good to have a very tight joint but proceed with caution. The spruce was measured like the cut on the body with each side extended. Once in place, the spruce is cut flush with the top and bottom of the sides. The ends of the spruce inlay will be covered by the soundboard and the back. Sand and scrape flush to the sides.

A very simple jig for excavating the material at the end graft can be constructed for routing. Decide the width at the top and at the bottom and the height and make a platform for a router or Dremel tool. The platform can be clamped to the instrument and the channel routed very accurately and quickly.

(Photo 9-7)   A nice view of the finished element.

End of Chapter 9

Chapter 10
The Bridge

There are two basic types of bridges found on ukuleles. These two bridges have many variations and is another way for a luthier to add a signature. All bridges have a removable saddle which is necessary to allow for adjustment of the heights of the strings above the fingerboard. The process of this adjustment will be discussed in chapter on *Set-up*. We will learn about pinned bridges and the tie block bridge by a bridge pin.

The pinned bridge has tapered wooden or plastic pins that bind the strings in a tapered hole that extend thru the bridge and the bridge patch. Steel string guitars have this type of bridge. A small knot is tied in the end of the string that will be held in the tapered hole in the bridge.

The tie block bridge is basically a bridge that has a slot for the saddle and a component that has hole drilled at the proper string spread for the instrument. Some strings are passed thru a hole with a knot that will hold the end of the string before passing over the saddle. Another variation is an arrangement of holes that allow the string to be tied with a knot that consists of several loops under itself called a surgeon's knot.

Ukuleles that are to be tuned to low G have compensation for the string's lengths in order to be able to properly tune the instrument. A pinned bridge is almost always used in this case and the slot for the saddle is at a mathematically calculated angle.

The wood used for the bridge is usually the same that is used for the fretboard. Most bridge blanks are approximately 1/4 **x** 1 **x** 4 inches. The saddle will be made of material that is 1/8 thick.

Procedure: Making a pinned bridge

The bridge blank for this bridge is 3/8 x 1 x 4 inches. The wood should match the wood used as the fretboard.

Step 1: Lay out saddle slot as per plan. This type bridge allow for string compensation. The angled saddle slot is easily routed using a simple jig using a Dremel tool or router.

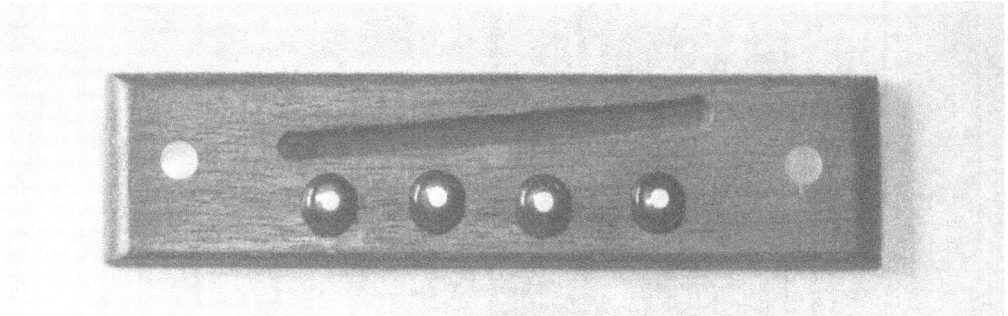

(**Photo 10-1**) A pin style bridge with rout for saddle & bridge pins

(**Photo 10-2**)   A simple jig to rout saddle slot

Step 2: Rout slot in bridge using Dremel tool and a 1/8 inch downcut router bit. The slot is centered side to side and is 2- 1/4 inches long and 3/16 inch deep. This cut should be made in several passes to prevent tear-out. When your bit is ready to plunge into the bridge blank, make every effort to hold the router vertical. The bit will want to move in the direction on the bit rotation so be prepared for that reaction.

(Photo 10-3) The saddle slot is routed

Step 3: The 13/64 inch holes that hold the strings and bridge pins are drilled in a straight line 1/4 inch from the back of the bridge. The holes should be chamfered slightly. The hole must be fitted to mate with the bridge pins, usually 5 degrees of taper. Using a reamer, taper the holes to accept the pins and strings. Check the size often and do not allow the whole to become to large for the bridge pins.

(**Photo 10-4**) A tapered reamer is used to form correct taper in bridge pin holes.

Procedure: Making a tie block bridge

Step 1: Starting with a 3/8 x 1 x 4 inch bridge blank, rip a 1/8 in groove centered at 5/16 inch from the fence 3/16 inch deep.

(**Photo 10-5**)   A variation of a tie block bridge

Step 2: Lay out centerline on back edge. The string spread is 1- 3/4 inch. Using dividers mark four evenly spaced marks 9/16 inch apart on the back edge. Using a small square mark the points across edge.

Step 3: Clamp bridge blank to another piece of hardwood one inch wide to use as a backer for drilling. Clamp the two pieces of wood for drilling on drill press.

Drill a 5/16 inch hole half way between the two pieces of wood at the marks 1/4 inch deep. See photo.

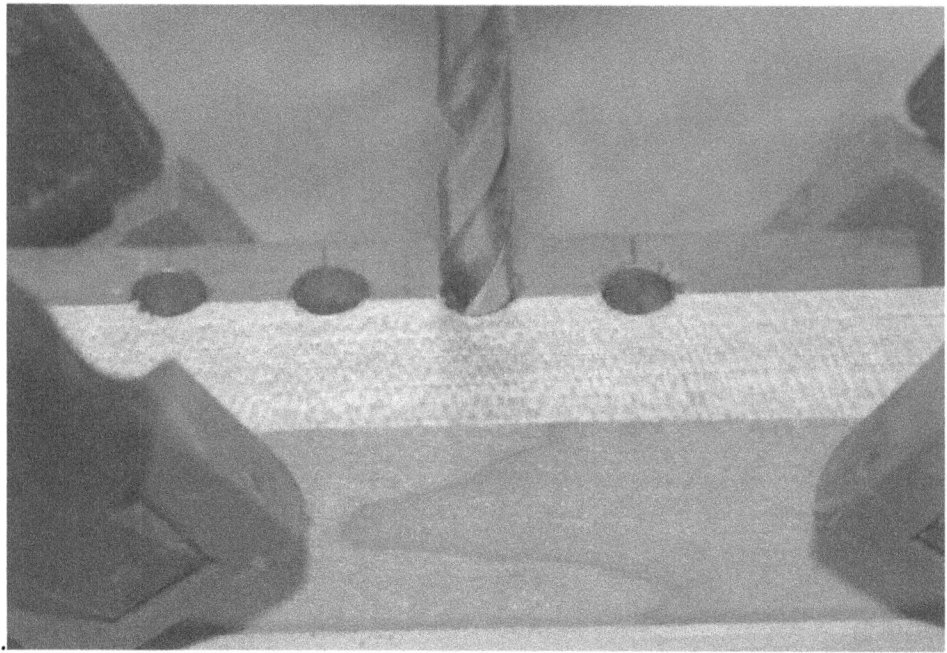

(**Photo 10-6**) Drilling the holes in the edge of bridge. The light colored wood is a maple backing for drilling the holes, the bridge is behind. The 5/16 inch holes are drilled half way between the two pieces of wood. Use a brad point bit.

(**Photo 10-7**)   Back side of bridge with half holes drilled

Step 4: Make small saw cuts in the middle of each half hole for strings to pass thru. A small knot is tied to prevent the string from being pulled thru saw cuts. Refer back to photo 10-4.

Step 5: Sand bottom of bridge dead flat and round over top edges slightly.

End of Chapter 10

Chapter 11
Locating Bridge

There are three dimensions that must be determined in order to align the bridge in the correct position. The distance of the centerline of the saddle to the front of the nut, the bridge must be perpendicular to the centerline of the ukulele, and the center of the bridge must be exactly on the centerline of the instrument. The bridge can be glued in place before or after finishing. Make light marks on all four sides with light lead pencil marks. If attached after the finish is applied, the area where the bridge will be located must be masked and all finish removed by scraping to allow glue to adhere properly. Most bridges start out about 1 inch x 4 inches for extra gluing surface. Do not ever add screws to the installation of the bridge.

Procedure: Locating Bridge

Step 1:

(**Photo 11-1**) Aligning the center of the bridge with the centerline of the ukulele.

Step 2: The bridge is located perpendicular to and on the centerline of the instrument. It is glued to the soundboard at a point where the centerline of the saddle is exactly 17 inches from the front of the nut. Refer to the section on *Jigs* to learn about a simple aid to help you attach the bridge at the correct position.

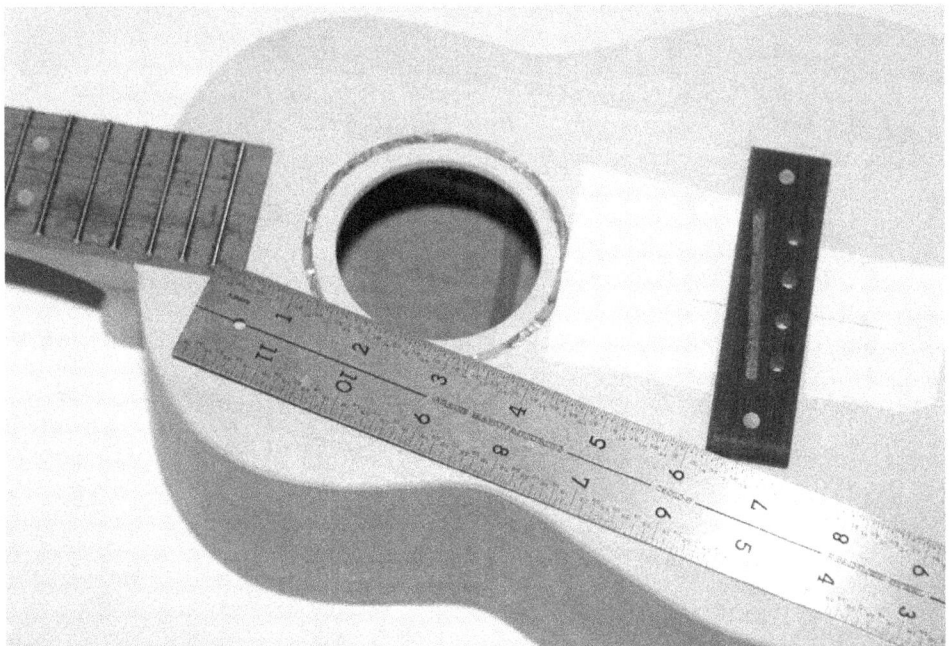

(**Photo 11-2**) Align bridge by measuring from the same point on each side of neck to the front corner of the bridge to check that bridge is perpendicular to the centerline of the ukulele.

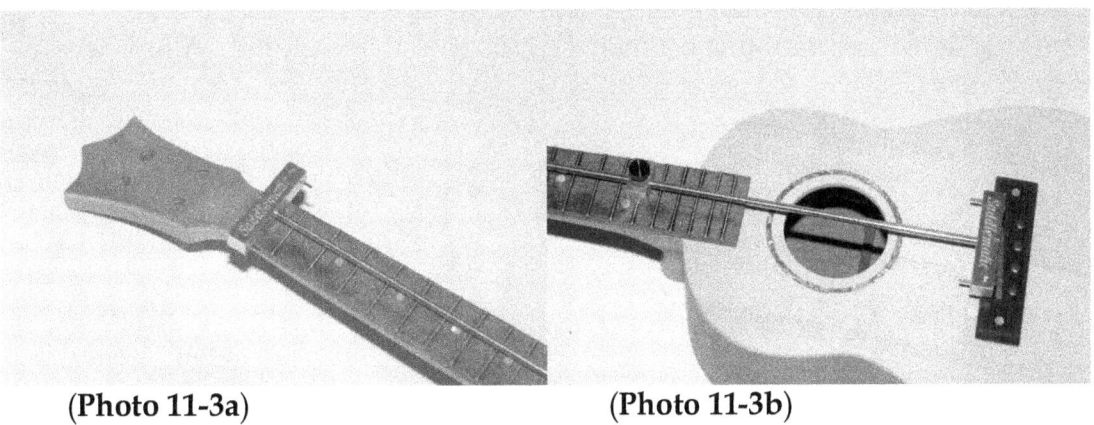

(**Photo 11-3a**)   (**Photo 11-3b**)

Step 3: Measuring the scale length is most easily done with the aid of an instrument that is set to the length from the front of the nut to the 12th fret. This is one half of the scale length. The instrument is turned 180 degrees and is set on the 12th fret and the other end now locates the bridge position. The sum total of these two lengths is equal to the scale length, or 17 inches. If you will be making a ukulele that is to tuned to low G, scale length compensation will be necessary. 5/32 inch should be added to the bass side of the saddle and 1/16 inch should be added to the treble side of the saddle. Confirm with your plan. (See *Jigs* section)

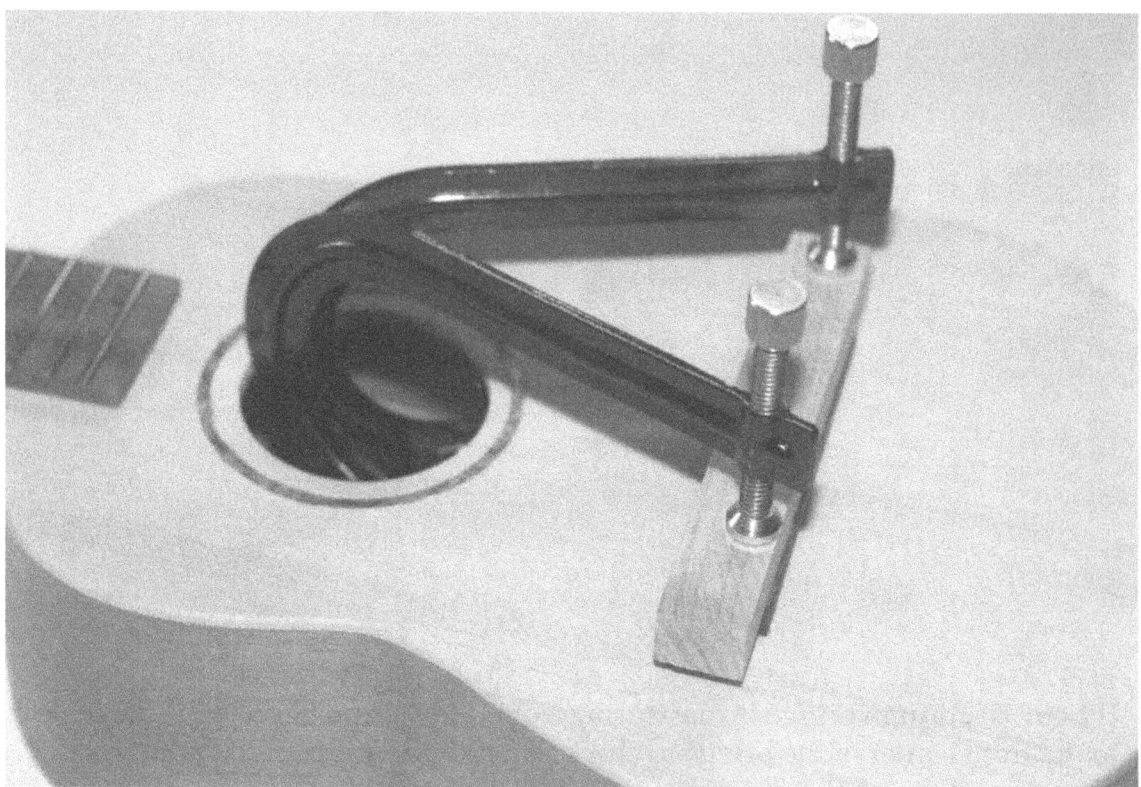

(**Photo 11-4**) The bridge is glued with Titebond and clamped using 2- 4 inch C clamps. There is not enough room in the soundhole to use more than two clamps so it is important that a 1 inch x 6 inch caul when gluing. Allow several hours to dry.

End of Chapter 11

Chapter 12
Binding

The edge banding strip on a ukulele is called the binding. Binding serves to add strength and protection to the edge of the instrument and serves to help seal the end grain of the soundboard. The binding can add an artistic element and demonstrate the builder's workmanship. Sometime the fretboard is also bound.

The binding can also include additional strips of thin wood laminated to add another dimension. These thin strips are known as purfling. The binding strips and the purfling strips are known collectively as binding. Each strip must have it's own ledge routed into the front and back edges of the ukulele. This is best done with a small router or Dremel tool. Depending on how detailed the binding and purfling there may be several ledges routed on the edges. When binding the fretboard, the width of the binding is subtracted from the width of the fretboard. Bindings and purflings can be woods, plastic or celluloid.

(**Photo 12-1**) The soundboard is best routed with the Dremel tool in it's router base. The top is flat and the router base gives more stability.

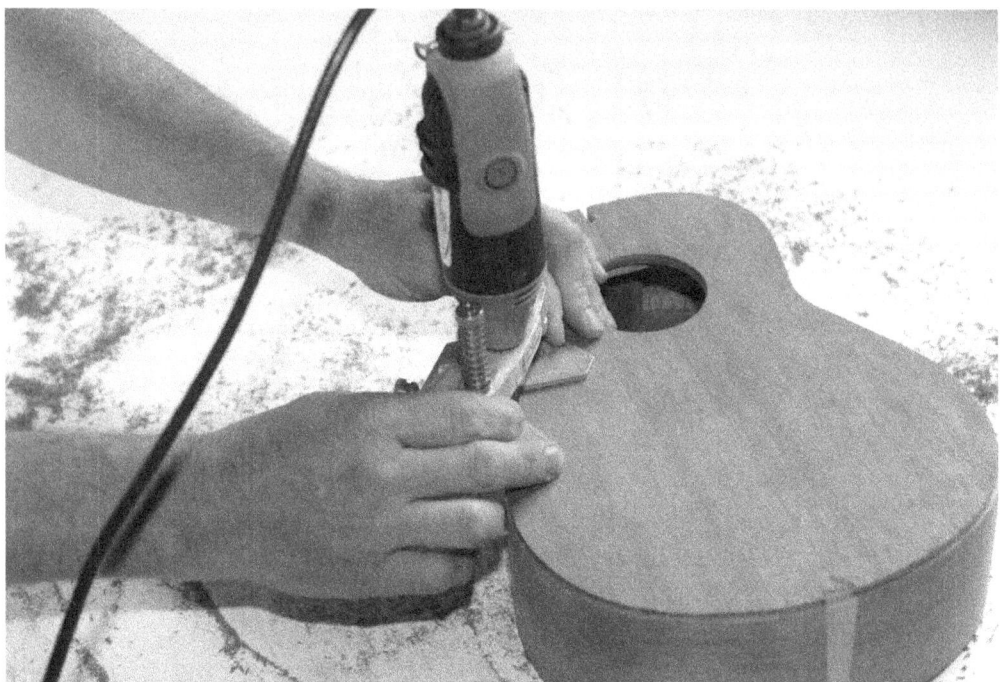

(**Photo 12-2**) Routing the ledge into the soundboard to accept the binding keeping the router base in constant contact with the soundboard and vertical.

(**Photo 12-3**) Routing the back for the binding strip. Hold the router guide as vertical as possible. There is not much bearing surface with this style of router base but it must be used because of the arch and taper built into the back of the instrument. The larger router base would not sit flat on the back and route a uneven channel.

(**Photo 12-4**) Since the back is arched and tapered, this type of router guide is often used. It's small bearing surface allows for a more precise cut but it is somewhat more difficult to use because of the small base. The width and the depth of the router cuts must me obtained by trial and error. You must make these settings on a test board and allow a small amount for the thickness of the adhesive used. When setting the depth and width of the cut, it is somewhat better to have the binding to project slightly rather than be sunken into the sides. If you can achieve a fit with approximately 1/32 inch of the binding proud that should be acceptable. The excess is scraped away later.

Practice with this type router guide. There is little contact with the top and it is most important that the tool be held in an exact vertical position. You must end up with a square cut so the binding will fit without gaps. The guide bearing should be kept at 180 degrees to the work piece and always keep the roller bearing the same distance from the cut. This will require turning the router carefully when routing the round parts of the body. Depending on the size of the binding, it may be necessary to rout the ledge in several passes. Make your last cut very small. If you make an unacceptable cut you can rout for a larger size binding.

Since some of the cuts are cutting the edge grain it is important to us a downcut router bit and make several shallow cuts to help prevent tear out.

(**Photo 12-5**) A close-up look at a properly routed ledge for a binding strip. If there are any places not routed properly, a chisel is used to clean up rough areas. Binding can also be installed with hand tools using a binding cutter and chisels. A binding cutter is a small hand tool of maple that has an adjustable cutting blade that is adjustable in depth and width. After the wood is scored with the small and very sharp blade the ledge is chiseled out by hand. Not an easy task but many people use this method.

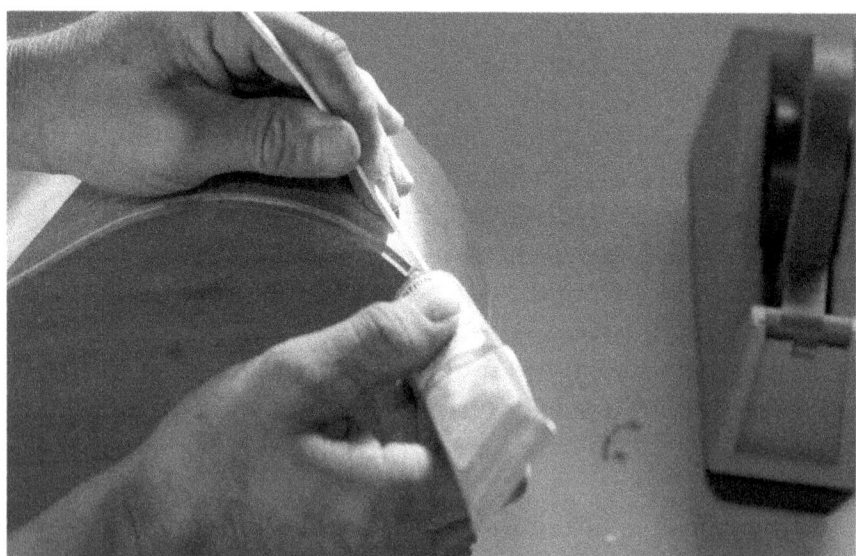

(**Photo 12-6**) Glue being applied to ledge and vinyl binding strip. Glue 8 to 10 inches at a time and the tape securely. (see **Photo 12-7**). Use a glue specifically made for vinyl to wood.

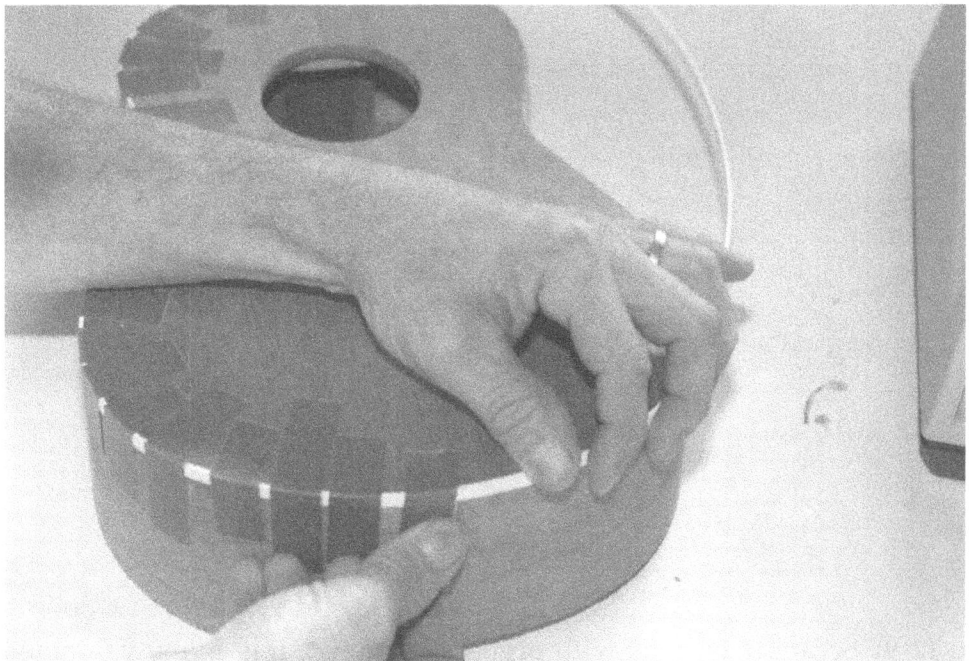

(**Photo 12-7**) Binding being held in place with strong tape. Apply tape at least every 1/4 inch. Press tape on soundboard first and with a firm downward pull cover binding, pushing inward and down, and firmly stick tape to side.

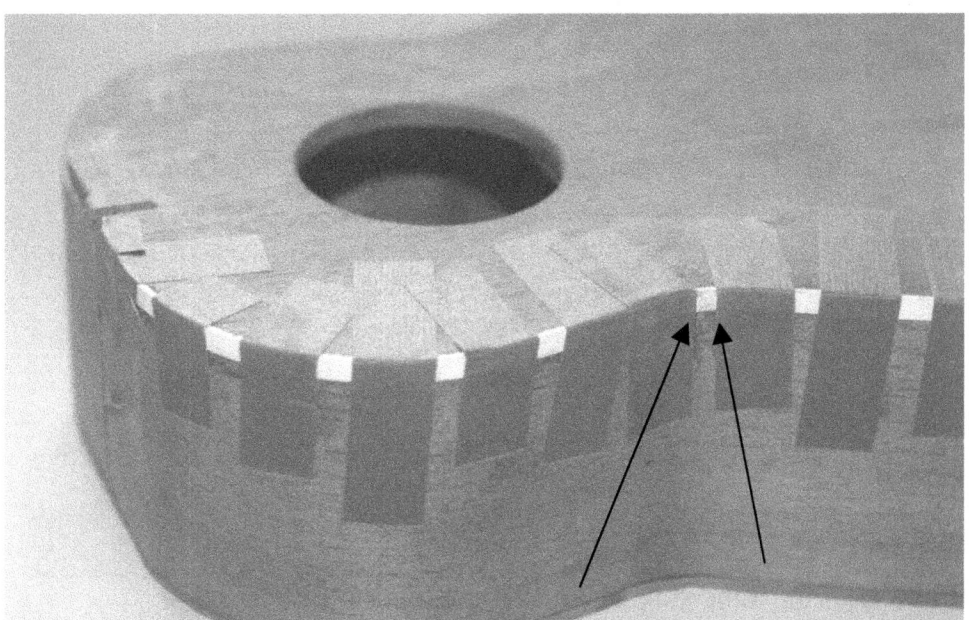

(**Photo 12-8**) Binding glued and taped. Give extra attention to the section around the waist area. If necessary use a small clamp across waist area.

(**Photo 12-9**) Scraping binding with prepared scraper. It is a very valuable tool for final preparation for finishing. There should be only a very slight difference between the surface of the side and the binding. A scraper is the best tool to level the two surfaces.

(**Photo 12-10**)   One side of binding scraped to final surface

End of Chapter 12

Chapter 13
Finishing

The most important reason for the finish on a ukulele is to protect it from our environmental moisture and to resist wear to the wood. The next most obvious reason it to enhance the beauty of out prized instrument. Today we have five reasonable type of finishes:

- Nitrocellulose Lacquer
- Water-based Lacquer
- Varnish
- Oil
- French Polish Shellac

It is way beyond the scope of this book to teach finishing techniques and there are many superb books on the subject. Collect information from many sources and experiment with some of the many resources that we have to us.

For our purposes we will discuss two types of oil finishes, Tru-Oil varnish and Watco Danish Oil. They are polimerized linseed oil with some additives. An oil finish is quite acceptable for a ukulele and will darken the color of most all woods. Mahogany becomes a rich medium dark finish and Sitka spruce will tend to have a slight amber cast. These colors are very pleasing. Some wood used for fretboards and bridges can be oiled the same way and at the same time as the rest of the instrument. We have used bubinga in building the two ukuleles for this book. Our choice of finishes for demonstration purposes was Watco Natural oil. Watco comes in many shades so check them out.

These oil finishes are extraordinarily safe and easy to use. There is no equipment required, just a couple of white cotton cloths. Masks and special ventilation is not a necessity but open, free moving air is best. Read and follow directions of the manufacturers.

Procedure: Applying Watco Danish oil finish

Step 1: Sand all surfaces to be oiled to 400 grit sandpaper and remove all dust with air gun or natural bristle brush. DO NOT us a tack cloth.

Step 2: Mask off all areas that are not to be oiled. Mask off soundhole. The interior of the instrument is not to be finished.

(Photo 13-1)   Initial application of oil

Step 3: Flood all surfaces with oil using a clean, white cotton cloth or a foam brush. Apply additional oil to areas that absorb the oil. Let the instrument to sit for about 30 minutes.

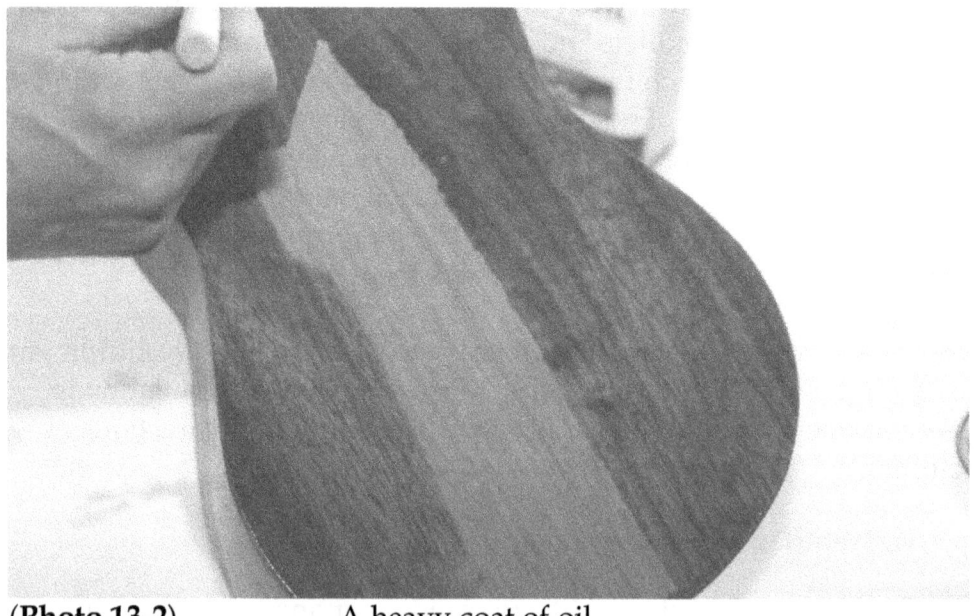

(Photo 13-2)   A heavy coat of oil

Step 4: Reapply oil and allow to penetrate for an additional 15 minutes. After 15 minutes wipe the surfaces dry with clean white cloth. Allow to dry 10 to 12 hours before use.

Step 5: Allow the instrument to dry a minimum of 72 hours in a climate controlled environment and top coat as desired. My choice is paste wax or Watco wax but the instrument can be sprayed with lacquers or polyurethane. Watco makes a wax that compliments their oils. It is an easy way to keep your ukulele looking good, just apply an occasional coat of this wax. It take about 10 minutes and will add a new luster to your instrument.

Any fretboard that cannot be oiled with Watco should be oiled with a special oil made to oil fretboards. Ebony and rosewoods fretboards must be oiled to prevent drying out and to help resist dirt and moisture using an oil made for this purpose.

(Photo 13-3)

The process of finishing an instrument with Tru-oil is the same as above but apply 6 or 8 coats of oil over several days.

End of Chapter 13

Chapter 14
Tuning Machines, Nut & Saddle

Procedure: Installation of tuning machines

The location of the tuning machines must allow the strings to go from the front of the nut directly to the tuning machine. When you design the shape of your headpiece keep this in mind. Do not allow the strings to touch other tuning machine posts.

There are two basic types of tuning machines. One is more like a peg on a violin and goes straight thru the headpiece. The other is a geared tuning machine and it is like the tuning machines used with guitars. The shaft is at 90 degrees to the headpiece. This style can have exposed or enclosed gears. Many tenor ukuleles use the geared type tuning machines.

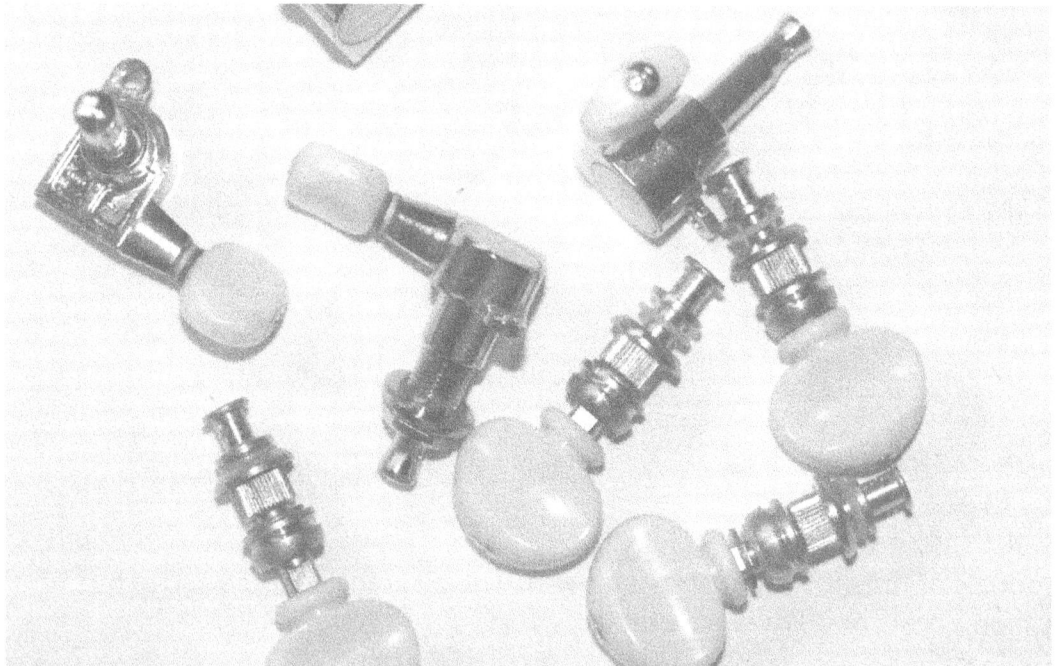

(**Photo 14-1**)   Tuning machines and Tuning pegs

Step 1: Clean the holes for the tuning machines to remove any finish residue or polishing compound. Check the fit and enlarge the holes with a tapered reamer checking the fit often.

Step 2: Insert the tuning machine from the bottom and slide the bushing over the shaft from the top. Add the washer and the nut and tighten finger tight.

Step 3: Align the tuning machines and mark the location of the small alignment holes. Drill a 1/16 inch pilot hole. Install the small screw but do not over tighten.

Procedure: Installing the Nut

The nut can be made out of many different materials. In the past bone was used often along with ebony. Now Corian, graphite, and many other man made materials are available. The thickness of if the nut for this tenor ukulele is 1/8 inch.

Step 1: Check the fit of the nut in the slot at the end of the fretboard. Do not be concerned with the height. Cut the nut material to width and sand to fit. Using a nut seating file, level the bottom of the nut slot. If the slot is too tight file slightly with fine file. If the nut is too thick, sand the nut but do not file the wood.

Procedure: Fitting the Saddle

The saddle, like the nut, can be made of bone, graphite, and Corian. Our saddle is 1/8 inch thick and should be cut to length with a saw and filed to shape. The saddle is about 2-1/4 inches long depending on the type bridge is used. Often if you buy a bridge blank for a guitar saddle you will have enough material to make the nut and saddle for a ukulele.

Step 1: Cut the saddle to length with a saw and file to shape. Do not be concerned with the height for now.

End of Chapter 14

Chapter 15
Set-up

The ukulele is ready to string up and play for the first time. The action, or how the instrument will play, is somewhat a trial and error process. The string spread at the nut is 1- 1/6 inch and at the saddle it is 1- 3/4 inch.

This discussion will be about the steps necessary to string and set the action on a tenor ukulele with a pin type bridge. The nut and saddle are finished to thickness and length and now we must establish the proper height of the strings above the frets.

Step 1: For the purpose of adjusting the nut and saddle we will install the 1st and 4th string. To do so with a pin bridge that uses bridge pins to secure the strings to the bridge, we must tie a knot in one end of the string. Try to tie the knots close to the end but with enough string to keep the knot from failing. The knot is a variation of the most basic overhand knot called "Surgeons Knot" It is an overhand knot with one or two extra loops of string through the middle of the knot. It provides for a somewhat larger knot that will be helpful with the bridge pins or slots. Tie this knot on strings one and four and insert them into the corresponding holes in the bridge. The knot is to pass all of the way thru the bridge and the bridge patch. The small groove in the bridge pin is for the string to pass thru to the saddle. Insert the string and slowly press the bridge pin into place. It should rest all of the way down to the top of the bridge.

Step 2: Lay a small 1/8 inch strip of wood across the saddle slot and the nut slot. Now that the string will have a reference point, pull first string tight over these strips and check the height of the string above the frets. If this distance is around 1/4 inch, use the 1/8 inch strip as a guide to mark across the nut and saddle. Sand the nut and saddle blank just short of this line. This is the beginning point of this trial and error process.

Step 3: Mark and notch the nut with the appropriate string spacing. See section on *Jigs*. Start a small groove at each point that the strings will pass over the nut with a small saw kerf. At this point, the top of the nut must slope away from the neck. A slope of 10 to 15 degrees is good with the front of the nut at the point above the point the nut touches the fretboard. This is to allow the string to touch in only at the front edge. If it were to the nut might be different for each the string. A definite point is necessary to be flat, the point of contact of string accurate.

Step 4: Insert the first string into the lower right tuning machine with the string winding on the inside of the shaft. Do the same with the forth string using the lower left tuning machine, winding from the inside also. Allow enough slack in the string to wind the string 3 to 4 revolutions.

Step 5: Tune to pitch and check the action. For "C" tuning the 1st (bottom) string is tuned to "A", second "E", third "G" and the forth string "C". The location of the string is marked on the envelope the string comes in and do not mix the strings up because they are not marked otherwise and the strings do not have any logic about their diameters. You will not be able to tune a tenor ukulele with an electronic guitar tuner because it is not the correct octave. However, if you put a capo on the fifth fret of a properly tuned guitar, the notes will be GCEA.

Very recently I found a chromatic tuner for guitar, bass, **and** ukulele. It is made by **Korg Model GT-12**. It is a chromatic tuner, automatic, manual and tone. It is in the $75 price range. See *Sources of Supplies*

There is always a pitch pipe. Also two of the websites in *Sources of Supplies* have tuner in their website. Use caution when tuning your ukulele and make sure that you are tuning your uke to the correct octave. If tuned to a higher octave you may put far too much tension on the strings. Something will have to give and most of the time it is the strings but not always. You may end up with a bridge in your hand.

End of Chapter 15

Jigs & Plans

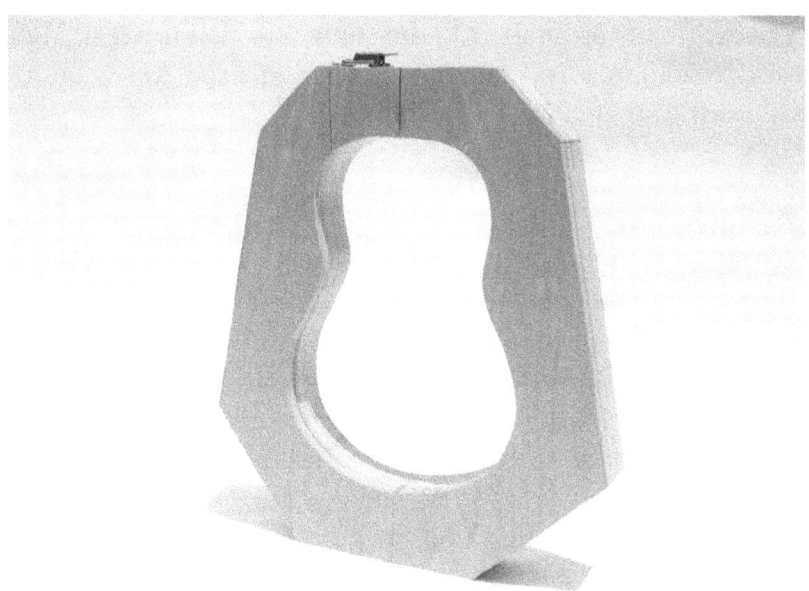

(Photo J-1)   Construction Mold- Box Style

These molds are made by laminating two pieces of 3/4 in plywood and cutting them to match the body template. Allow for the thickness of the sides when cutting to form. The entrance cut on the box style mold is kept closed with a luggage clasp. The cut us necessary aid in removing the glued up body from the mold. Simply insert a small screwdriver in the cut to pry the mold open slightly. This is the single most important jig.

Procedure: Making Construction Mold

Step 1: Laminate 3 pieces of 3/4 inch plywood 16 inches x 18 inches. This is best done by securing one piece of plywood to another with 1-1/4 inch drywall screws without any glue. Next screw the third piece of plywood to one side, still no glue. After the body template shape is sawed the three pieces of plywood are unscrewed and then glued and the screws replaced until the glue is dry. Do not leave any screws in the mold. By sawing the shape out of the plywood you save much glue and time.

Step 2: Establish a centerline along the long side and extend it to both ends and the back. Using the centerline trace the outline of the body from the template (see *Plans* section. This template does not allow any room for the width of the sides so you must add this dimension to the template before you saw the mold.

Step 3: With a band saw or sabre saw cut the outline of the body just inside the outline. Sand to line. Remove all remaining screws and cut away unnecessary wood around the cutout. See photos *J-1* & *J-2*.

Step 4: Install a luggage draw clasp over the cut into the cutout. This is to secure the mold while in use.

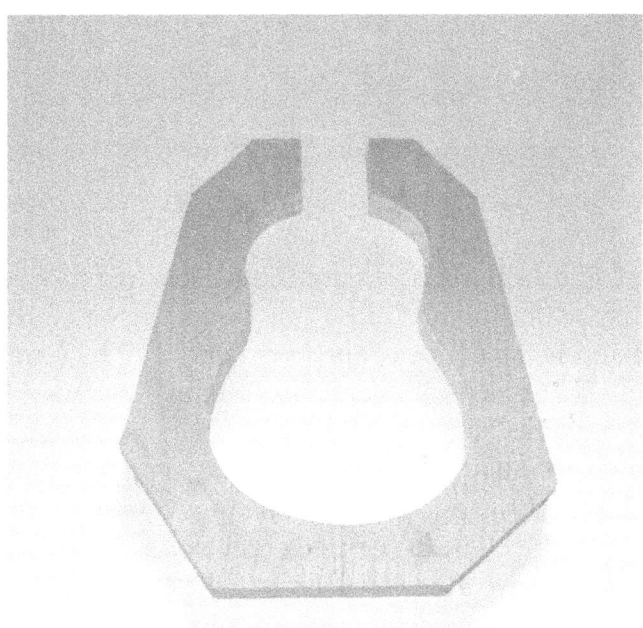

(**Photo J-2**)   Construction Mold- Spanish Style

(Photo J-3)   Alignment/Gluing jig for Spanish style neck construction

This jig is necessary to attach the neck and the three cauls moves as necessary to align the body to neck after the heelblock has been attached. The jig is made of 3/4 inch plywood and is the shape of the body plus 1/2 inch and the arms that are used to clamp the cauls are 6 inches. The long arm is about 18 inches for an overall length of 36 inches. The work form can be screwed or clamped to the work table for ease of access around the jig. The cauls are laminated from 4 layers of 3/4 inch birch plywood. They can be move to any angle and are held in place with clamps. The block in the center of the soundhole is used to clamp the braced soundboard to the jig. It is 3/4 x 1 x 3 inches. Establish and mark a centerline on the jig.

(Photo J-4)   Jig in use gluing neck

Plate Gluing Jig

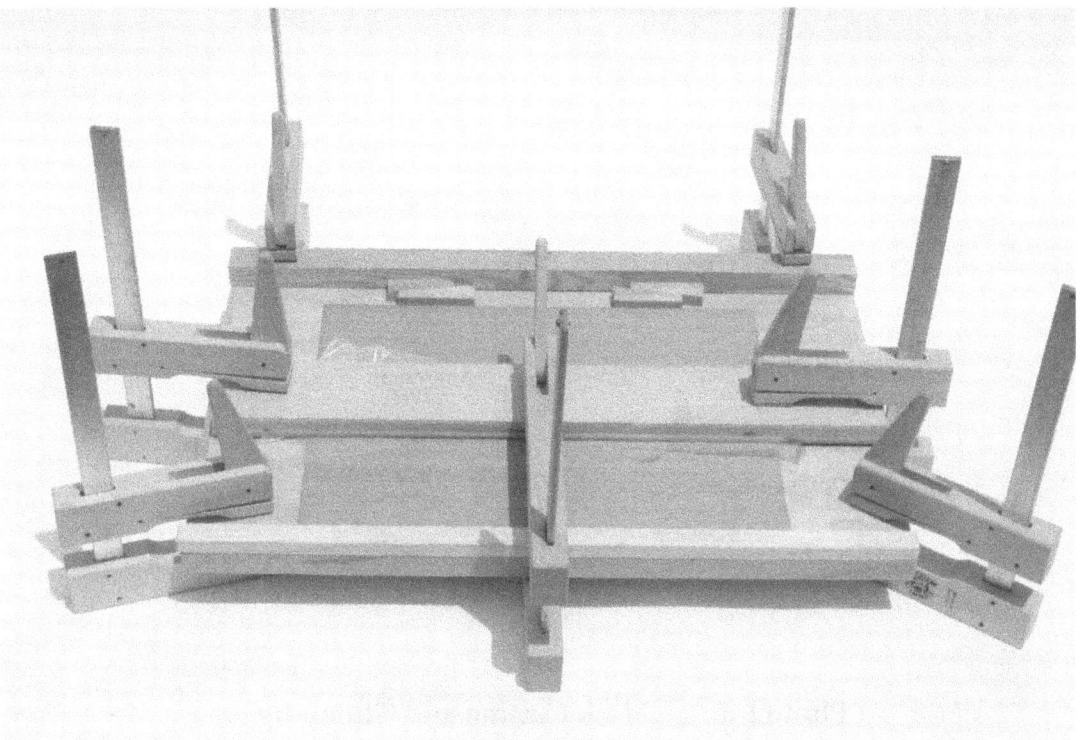

(Photo J-5)   Plate Gluing Jig

This jig is necessary to glue the two halves of the soundboard and back together It allows for a perfect joint. The halves are forced together with the use of wedge sand a fixed stop. The jig consists of a base that is about 14 inches x 20 inches and has a 1/2 x 3/4 x 20 inch strip glued flush to one side. Another strip of 3/4 inch plywood that is movable and clamped in place for the size of plates being joined. Another strip of 3/4 inch plywood is used to clamp the seam of the two halves. There is a strip of wax paper above and below the joint. Two pair of 2 inch long wedges are needed to use as clamps that press against the movable strip that act as clamps. The extra clamps in front are used to level the base.

To use the jig, place the two halves on the base and adjust and clamp the movable fence to within about 1 inch of the edge of the plates. Use the small opposing wooden wedges to exert pressure on the two halves. Place the second plywood strip over the joint and clamp in two places. Remove from jig and glue with Titebond. Clamp and allow to dry several hours.

(**Photo J-6**)   Neck Cutting and Gluing Jig

Step 1: Start with a piece of 3/4 inch plywood 9 inches x 15 inches. At a point 4 inches from the left side draw a line 15 degrees from front to back.

Step 2: Make a fence board from a piece of 3/4 inch maple or poplar 2-1/2 x 15 inches. (two pieces of 3/4 inch plywood glued together will work also)

Step 3: Cut three triangle blocks with two legs 2-1/4 inches from maple or poplar to use as braces.

Step 4: Glue the fence board along one side of the line drawn at 15 degrees from the front. Next, glue the three 2-1/4 inch braces at 90 degrees to the fence board. It is most important that the fence board is 90 degrees to the base.

To use the jig adjust the fence on a band saw or table saw to cut thru the jig near the fence. Clamp neck blank to the fence board of the jig.

Procedure: Making Side Sanding Board

(Photo J-7)   Side Sanding Board

Step 1: Cut a piece of 3/4 inch plywood to 12 inches x 18 inched. Also cut one piece of 3/4 inch plywood to 2-1/2 x 12 inches and one piece 2-1/12 x 18 inches.

Step 2: Center and glue the 2-1/2 inch x 18 inch plywood strip flush with one of the short sides. Glue the 2- 1/2 x 12 inch strip to the opposite end flush with the edge of baseboard.

Step 3: Glue a 12 inch x 18 inch sheet of 80 grit sandpaper to the top. Large sandpaper is available at home improvement store that is used with floor sanders. If this sandpaper is not available, use cut strips of sandpaper belts used for belt sanders

This sanding jig is designed to be used on a flat surface adjacent to the edge of a work table. The two extensions of plywood at one end are used to clamp the jig to the work table.

Shooting Board

(Photo J-8)   Shooting Board

Procedure: Construction of a Shooting Board

Step 1: Starting with piece of 3/4 inch plywood 12 inches x 30 inches. Glue and screw a piece of 3/4 inch plywood 9 inches x 30 inches flush with one side of the first piece of plywood.

Step 2: Glue and screw a piece of 3/4 inch plywood 2 inches x 9 inches on the right end. This will serve a stop and should be square to the ledge formed by the 9 inch x 30 inch piece of plywood.

Step 3: Cut and attach two 2 inch x 30 inch strips of 3/4 inch birch plywood to the bottom parallel to the edges 1 inch from each side.

Step 4: Cut and sand a piece of 3/4 inch birch plywood 2 inches x 30 inches to be used as a hold down board that can be clamped into position when needed.

Step 5: Make a sanding block from a block of wood, maybe a very straight section of a 2x4 about 16 inches long. The tall side must be at 90 degrees to the base. Double check when you have prepared the wooden block and before you apply the sandpaper. 120 grit or 150 grit will be good. You will find many other uses for this sanding block and you might want to make several in different lengths and grades of sandpaper. **Photo J-8** shows a pair of plates ready to be sanded or planed.

Procedure: Building Fret Saw Jig

Step 1: The jig consists of a base with two flat sides that create a way for the fretboard to slide under a guide block. The base is 3/4 inch birch plywood 7 inches x 14 inches and a 1/2 x 2 x 14 inches is glued flush and flat on each side.

Step 2: The guide block should be cut from solid wood, maybe maple. The height of the guild block will be determined by the size of the saw, thickness of the fretboard, and the depth of the fret kerf.

Step 3: The jig should be used only to cut fret kerfs with a fret saw. The kerf of a fret saw is usually .024 inches. You must preserve the saw kerf as a measuring point for spacing the kerfs.

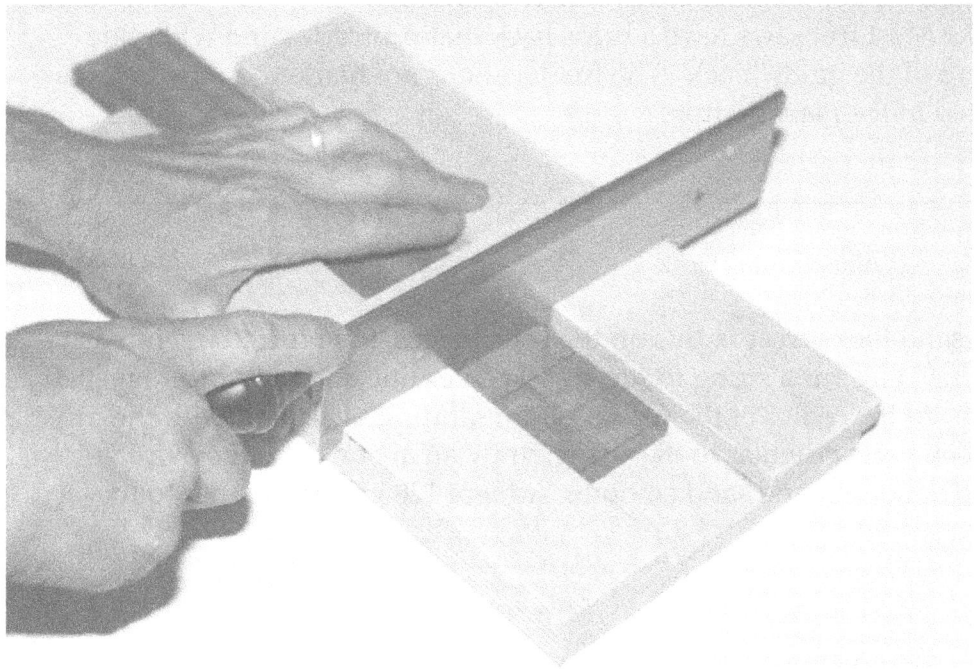

(Photo J-9)　　　　　　　　Fret Slot Cutting Jig

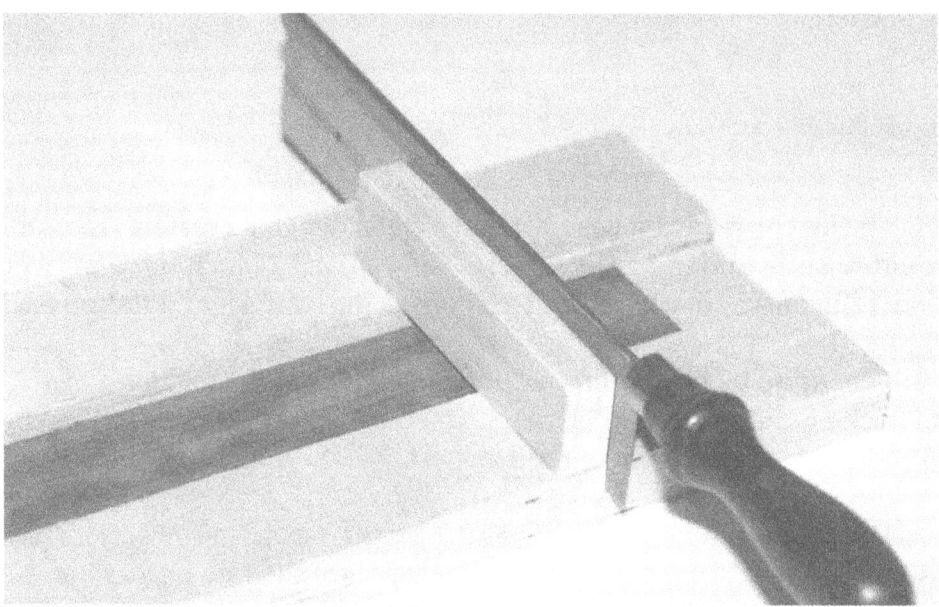

(Photo J-10)   The left side of the jig

Step 4: Adjust the depth of cut using veneer or thin strips of wood on top of the guide block. Most fret saws have a brass back that protrudes and will glide along the top of the guide block. The fret locations are marked on the fretboard and are listed in the *Plans* section.

Procedure: Making radius sanding block

Step 1: To sand the correct radius on the back braces, they must be sanded at a 15 foot radius. Lay out a string to serve as a center line and measure 15 feet and drive a nail. At the center of the wood for the sanding block and with the sanding block perpendicular to the string, draw an arc on the edge of a 18 inch 2x4. Saw on band saw and sand smooth. Adhere 120 grit sandpaper to the face of the block.

(Photo J-11)   15 Foot Radius Sanding Block

Procedure: Side Bending Jig

(**Photo J-12**) A side view of the Side Bending Jig. The heat is from a silicone blanket that is sandwiched between a flexible steel form and the wooden side being bent.

(**Photo J-13**)   Front view of Side Bender

The body template is used to transfer the exact shape of the sides. Allow for the thickness of the sides. Threaded rods with large threaded knobs tighten the cauls and bend the sides with heat and water.

Procedure: Saddle Location Jig:

The scale length for this tenor ukulele is 17 inches. This jig will allow you to accurately locate the bridge and saddle. It consists of a beam 1/4"x 3/4 x 14 inches piece of maple, a 1/4 x 1/4 x 2 inch cross piece and two small lengths of round toothpicks.

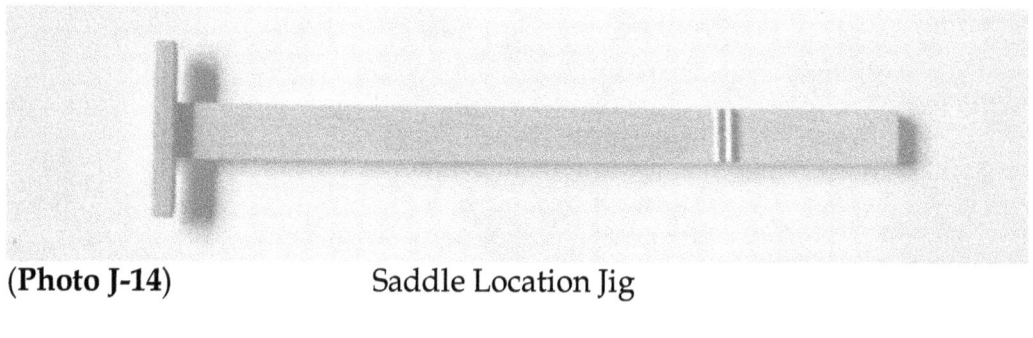

(Photo J-14)   Saddle Location Jig

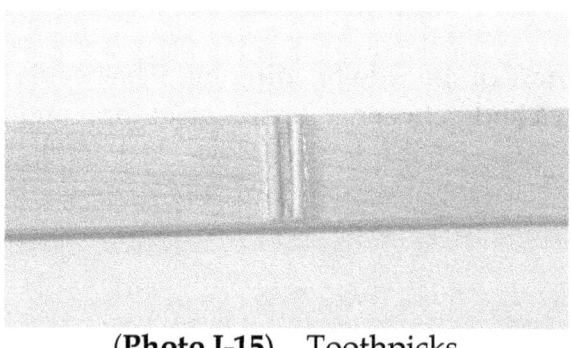

(Photo J-15)   Toothpicks

The cross piece is glued at 90 degrees to the beam, flush at the end of the beam. The toothpicks are glued exactly on each side of the 12th fret. Sand flush and edges and ends.

Procedure: Sliding Table Jig/ Neck Nibbler

(**Photo J-17**)   Top View

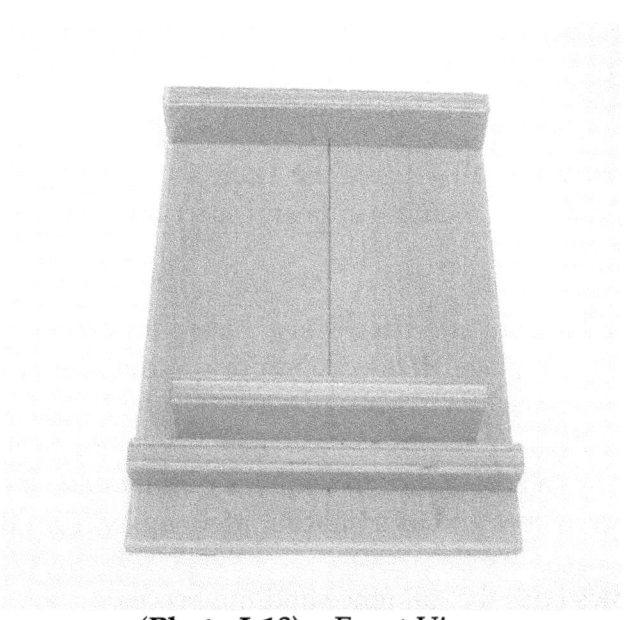

(**Photo J-18**)   Front View

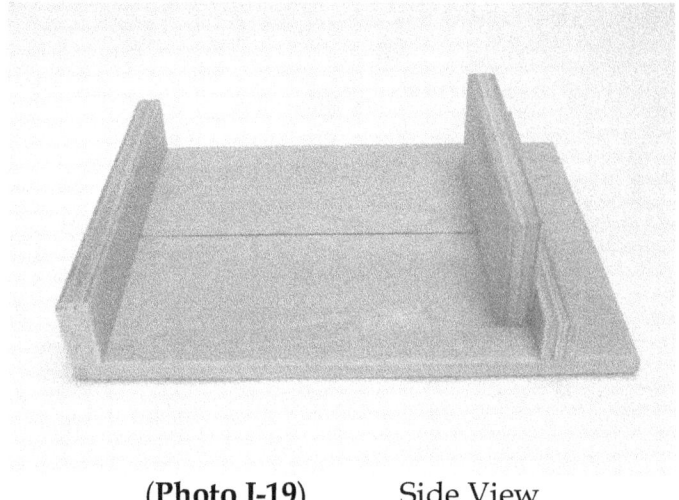

(**Photo J-19**)   Side View

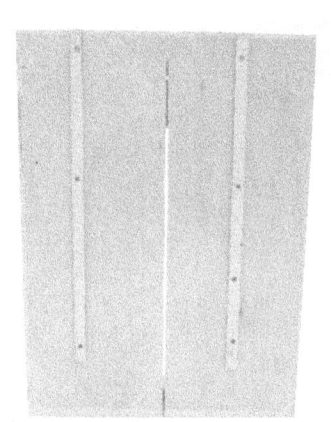

(**Photo J-20**)   Bottom View

Photos **J-17** thru **J-20** Show all sides of the Table Saw Sliding Table. It is intended to help make very accurate cuts and safer cuts on the table saw for certain procedures.

The Top View shows a front and back brace that spans across the table. It should be glued and screwed in place. It is very important that the braces are exactly perpendicular to the centerline. This will serve as a fence for your work.

The Front View shows a taller fence in the back of the table. It is added to aid in supporting tall work pieces and as a handle safely away from the blade.

The Side View shows both the tall fence and the braces.

The Bottom View shows the two maple runners sized to fit in the grooves for a mitre gauge in the table of the saw. You must align and attach the runners so the table moves smoothly across the saw table and guided by these two strips.

Notice that the sliding table is cut almost from end to end and that is why the front and back braces play and important role in holding this jig together.

This jig is almost a necessity to properly align and cut the neck and soundbox when making the slots for the biscuit to align the two components. This sliding table is what is used to set up and use the *Neck Nibbler*.

The table is 18 inches x 24 inches and is made of birch plywood for strength and stability. The front and back braces are 3 inches tall and 1- 1/2 thick. The taller back fence is 6 inches tall and 1- 1/2 wide.

Bill of Materials
Tenor Ukulele

-1 set of soundboards and back-- two bookmatched sets 10"x14" min. and
-1 set of sides 3 1/2 x 22 inches
-1 Honduran mahogany neck blank   1" x 3"x 28"
     or 7/8"x 2"x 18", 2- 7/8 x 2" heel blocks and 2 head extensions
-Tailblock H. Mahogany 13/16"min. x 2"x 3"
-Bridge patch 3/32"x 1-1/4" x 1"
-Soundhole patch 3/32"x 3-3/4" x 3-3/34"
-Kerfing small- approximately 80 inches- spruce or H. mahogany
-Bracewood 5/16" x 3/8"- 4 pieces 14" long, spruce
-Fretboard-Bubinga or other 1/4"x 2" x 13"
-Bridge blank to match fretboard 1/4+"x 1"x 4"
-Tuning machines- mini, geared
-Nut & Saddle material- 1/8"
-Fret wire -narrow crown -4'
-MOP Fretboard markers

Material for Jigs

3/4" birch plywood - 1 sheet
Titebond glue
1- 1/4" drywall screws
Maple or poplar -2 bf

Sources of Supplies

Ukulele Supply of Hawaii
95-421 Kuahelani Avenue #127
Mililani, HI 96789
Phone 808-625-7188
UkeSupply@Hawaii.RR.com

Koa & Other Hawaiian Woods, Inlay Material, Parts, Bending Blankets, Jigs and Kits

Highland Hardware
1045 North Highland Avenue, NE
Atlanta, GA 30306
800-241-6748
Highlandhardware.com

Fine Woodworking Tools, Handmade Wood Rasps, Chisels, Japanese Saws
Very Nice Catalog

Stewart-MacDonald
21 N. Shafer Street
Athens, Ohio 45701
800-848-2273
stewmac.com

Many special tools, parts, wood, finishes
General Luthier Supplies

Luthiers Mercantile International, Inc
7975 Cameron Drive, Bldg 1600
Windsor, CA 95492
800-477-4437
www.lmii.com

Wood, tuners, bridges, fretwire, tools finishing supplies, and much more
Complete Catalog

Luthimate
5, Rue des Bois
89140 MICHERY
FRANCE
+33 (0)386 67 05 95
www.luthimate.fr

Full line luthier supply--tuners, tools pickups, clamps, wood, plans, books
Very nice Website. Serving Europe

Websites to Visit:

UkuleleBooks.com.

Beatlessite.info/index.html

Ukuleleguild.org

ukuleles.com

Frets.com

Suggested Reading

Guitarmaking
Tradition and Technology
by: William R. Cumpiano,
Jonathan D. Natelson

137

Fret Scale

17 inch Tenor Ukulele

Fret	Distance
Fret 1 =	0.954
Fret 2 =	1.855
Fret 3 =	2.705
Fret 4 =	3.507
Fret 5 =	4.264
Fret 6 =	4.979
Fret 7 =	5.654
Fret 8 =	6.291
Fret 9 =	6.892
Fret 10 =	7.459
Fret 11 =	7.995
Fret 12 =	8.500
Fret 13 =	8.977
Fret 14 =	9.427
Fret 15 =	9.852
Fret 16 =	10.253
Fret 17 =	10.632
Fret 18 =	10.989

Measurements from Nut in Inches
The frets are measured in inches from the front of the nut to the centerline of the saw kerf. The width of a common fret saw blade is .024 inches.

UKULELE Design & Construction

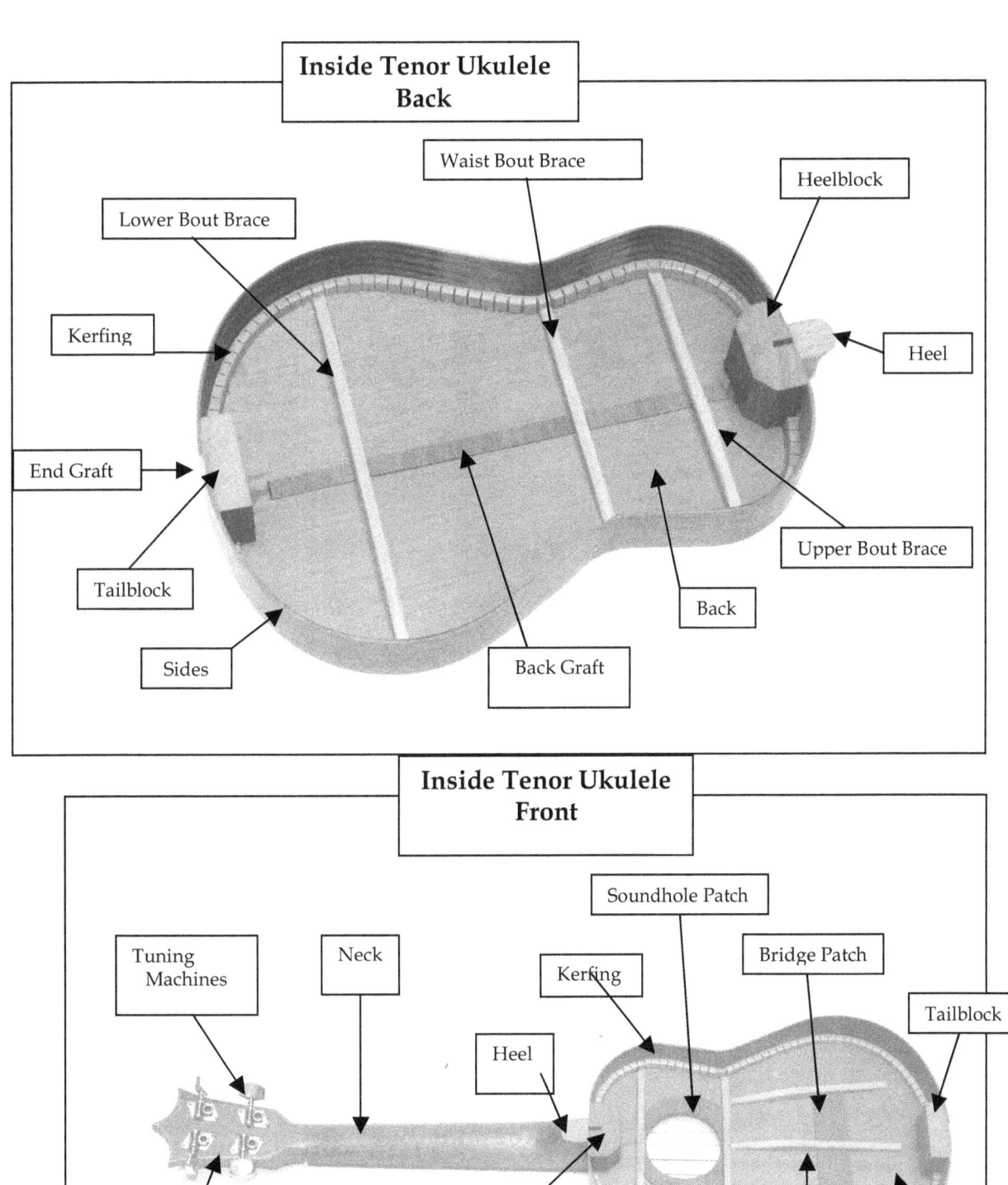

UKULELE Design & Construction

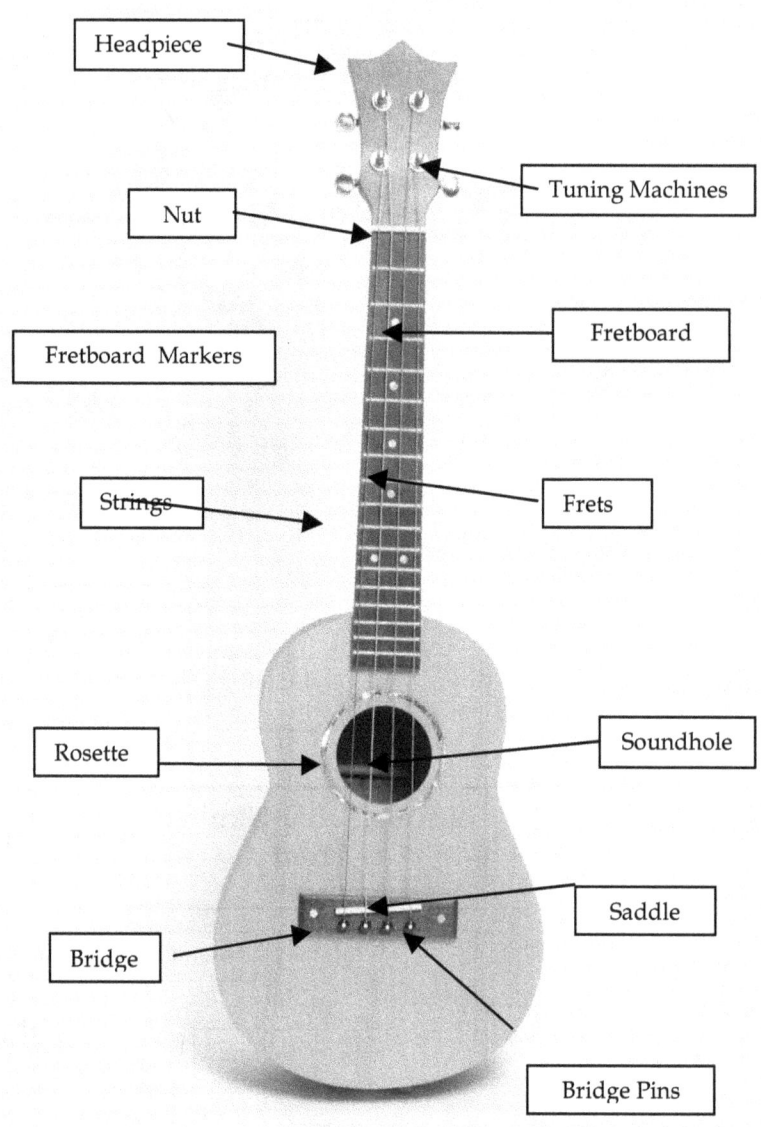

Tenor Ukulele

140

UKULELE Design & Construction

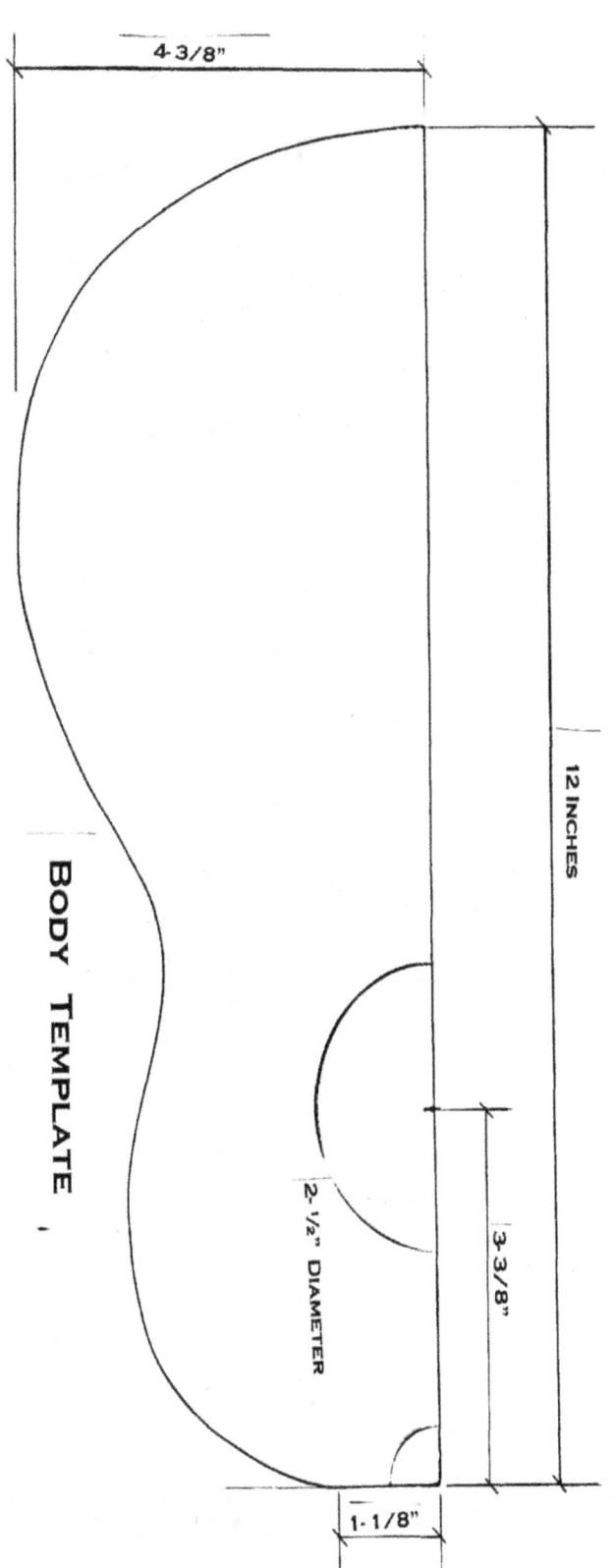

Body Plan
Enlarge to size

UKULELE Design & Construction

To obtain additional copies
visit your local bookstore or order online at

UkuleleBooks.com

Books are $24.95 each plus $5.85 for shipping.
Full Size Working **Plans** are 10.95 plus $1.85 Media Mail
Your books will be sent to you via Priority Mail within the USA. International shipping is extra. Please contact us for information.
E-mail: info@UkuleleBooks.com

Visit us at
UkuleleBooks.com
to order additional copies

We offer quantity discounts for bulk purchases of this book and plans.

Prices subject to change without notice
January 2006

www.ingramcontent.com/pod-product-compliance
Lightning Source LLC
Chambersburg PA
CBHW080548170426
43195CB00016B/2719